Teach® Yourself

Co[illegible]
Writing Success

Bekki Hill

Hodder Education

338 Euston Road, London NW1 3BH.

Hodder Education is an Hachette UK company.

First published in UK 2011 by Hodder Education.

First published in US 2011 by The McGraw-Hill Companies, Inc.

This edition published 2011.

British Library Cataloguing in Publication Data: a catalogue record for this title is available from the British Library.

Library of Congress Catalog Card Number: on file.

10 9 8 7 6 5 4 3 2 1

The publisher has us[illegible]at any website addresses referred to in this book are correct and active at the time of going to press. However, the publisher and the author have no responsibility for the websites and can make no guarantee that a site will remai[illegible]that the content will remain relevant, decent or appropriat[illegible]

The publisher has made every effort to mark as such all words which it believes to be trademarks. The publisher should also like to make it clear t[illegible] whether marked or u[illegible], in no way affects its legal status as a trademark.

Every reasonable effort has been made by the publisher to trace the copyright holders of [illegible] in this book. Any errors or [illegible] should be notified in writing to the publisher, who will endeavour to rectify the situation for any reprints and future editions.

Hachette UK's policy is to use papers that are natural, renewable and recyclable produ[illegible] and made from wood grown in sustainable forests. The logging and manufacturing processes are expected to conform to the environmental regulations of the country of origin.

www.hoddereducation.co.uk

Typeset by MPS Limited, a Macmillan Company.

Printed in Great Britain by CPI Cox & Wyman, Reading.

Disclaimer

You're solely responsible for the way you view and use the information in this book, and do so at your own risk. The author and publisher are not responsible in any way for any kind of injuries or health problems that might occur due to using this book or following the advice in it.

Acknowledgements

Many thanks to all the people who supported me in creating this book. Particular thanks go to Addy Farmer, Benjamin Scott, Chris Smith, Gill Smith, Juliet Clare Bell, Nicky Schmidt, Sue Hyams and Wendy Barton who generously commented on my work in progress.

I would also like to thank the writers who completed The Write Coach survey on 'writer's block' and procrastination, and the writers who kindly gave their time to answer my questionnaires and allowed me to quote them within the text. I only wish I had more space to use all of their insightful comments.

My biggest thanks, however, go to my husband Steve for his support both in creating this book and in all my coaching and writing endeavours.

Finally, thank you to everyone at Hodder who made this book a reality.

Image credits

Front cover: © Grove Pashley/Stockbyte/Getty Images

Back cover: © Jakub Semeniuk/iStockphoto.com, © Royalty-Free/Corbis, © agencyby/iStockphoto.com, © Andy Cook/iStockphoto.com, © Christopher Ewing/iStockphoto.com, © zebicho – Fotolia.com, © Geoffrey Holman/iStockphoto.com, © Photodisc/Getty Images, © James C. Pruitt/iStockphoto.com, © Mohamed Saber – Fotolia.com

Contents

Meet the author

Welcome to *Coach Yourself to Writing Success!*

When I was involved in a car crash that left me struggling to recover from my injuries, my confidence hit an all-time low and I abandoned my dreams of becoming a published writer. In my endeavours to regain my confidence, I discovered life coaching and was so impressed by the methods it used to turn people's lives around, I trained to become a life coach.

Coaching also enabled me to rekindle my passion for writing, to deal with the rejections that followed, beat the moments of self-doubt and enhance my creativity. This led me to recognize that coaching techniques could be adapted to help writers create strong strategies for success and address perennial writing challenges such as writers' block, loss of motivation, procrastination, lack of time and rejection.

In 2003 I founded The Write Coach and began assisting both professional and aspiring writers to overcome their challenges and to become more successful. Since then I have personally coached hundreds of writers, developed a coaching component for an MA in Screenwriting and, for over five years, I wrote a motivation column in writing magazine *Mslexia*.

As a writer I have published short stories and non-fiction features. I've also published this book, which I hope helps other writers and aspiring writers to transform their dreams into reality. For further inspiration you can also visit my website, www.thewritecoach.co.uk and follow me on twitter @bekkiwritecoach.

Bekki Hill, 2011

1 In one minute

All too often great writers fail to achieve their potential because they are daunted by thoughts that suffocate their motivation, gag their creativity, encourage procrastination and leave them questioning if they're wasting their time writing. Even when things are going well, negativity drifts through our minds; thoughts such as:

'My writing's not good enough.'

'What if I get stuck?'

'I haven't got the time.'

'I should be doing something else.'

'It's just too hard to break into publishing.'

Becoming a successful writer, in any field, is a real challenge. If we listen to the voices of negativity, we make it even harder. Yet it isn't just negativity that stands in the way of success. Positive thoughts can easily lead you in the wrong direction, too.

Coaching enables you to address your thinking; both the obviously unhelpful thoughts and those that sneak under the radar whispering disbelief or leading you astray. Coaching shows you how to turn these thoughts around, so instead of slowing you down and holding you back, your thinking speeds you on and equips you to deal with the challenges you face.

Introduction

On the surface all writers appear to face the same set of challenges: procrastination, loss of motivation, lack of creativity, blocks, loss of confidence, rejection and lack of time. Underlying these is the conundrum of getting your work published or performed. Yet, while writers' challenges may be very similar, the root causes, and therefore the solutions to overcoming them, will be unique to each individual.

Coaching facilitates the discovery of personal strategies that work for the individual. It is therefore a highly effective tool for assisting writers to identify unique personal solutions to their challenges and to achieving success.

The way you employ this book will depend on what you wish to gain from it.

Using this book as a coaching programme

By working your way through Part one, you can identify your writing goals, develop strong strategies to achieve them and work on the thought processes that underpin your chances of success. Part two will help you to increase motivation and creativity. Working with parts one and two will also make a significant contribution to evading the persistent challenges many writers encounter. Part three will give you further insight into specific writing concerns that you may have, assist you in addressing them and learning how to avoid encountering them in future.

If you use the book in this way, you will need:

- **A contemplation journal** – this is for you to do specific exercises in, to discuss thoughts and ideas and make notes of things you need to remember.
- **An achievement log** – use your achievement log to keep track of what you have accomplished and what you plan to achieve. You will be told when you need to use this.

Using this book to address your challenges

This book can also be used to pinpoint challenges you are currently facing and identify ways to overcome them. If you work in this way, check the contents list from Chapter 6 onwards and choose the parts that resonate with the challenges you are experiencing.

If you're using this book to troubleshoot particular challenges, you may have little call for a contemplation journal (explained earlier) and may not even need an achievement log (also explained earlier). The need for these will depend on what challenges you work on.

Whatever way you choose to work with this book

To gain the best value from the exercises, you should also bear the following in mind:

- When you answer any questions, be as honest as you can. Don't hold back because something seems silly or unachievable. Don't look for the 'right' answer. This book is not about being right, it's about being you.
- The questions are designed to address a variety of underlying causes that create perennial writers' challenges and assist the reader to recognize thoughts that are sometimes unique to them. Therefore, there may be the odd question that seems irrelevant to you. If there is, answer the question exactly as it is asked. If, having answered a question (or attempted to), you still can't see the relevance, move on. It probably isn't for you.
- Occasionally two questions may appear to be asking the same thing – they aren't. They are carefully worded to gain different angles on your thinking. However, sometimes when we take a different angle, we still find the same answer. If you feel you're being asked the same question twice, check that you've answered the questions exactly as they are asked. If they still produce the same answers, then that's simply the way it works for you.
- When you've done whatever work you want to do in this book, take a look at Chapter 15. This chapter will assist you to devise a personal plan to ensure the changes you make really impact on your writing success.

Part one
Building the foundations of success

Introduction to Part one

The Foundations for a better tomorrow must be laid today.

Anon

To achieve and maintain success we need to build from the bottom up. In coaching we accomplish this using the three foundation stones of:

- ***what you want***
- ***who you are***
- ***what you think.***

What you want

Identifying and clarifying what you want to achieve is a vital step for anyone who wishes to enhance their chances of success. Using coaching tools and exercises to consider your long-distance plans, then shifting your focus to greater detail, can help you to:

- build better, more sustained focus on your writing and your writing goals
- increase your motivation to write
- save time
- reduce procrastination and indecision
- prevent the mind-jam that can develop when you work on large writing projects.

Who you are

Looking at ourselves in the mirror can be very powerful. When you work on 'who you are', you may feel as though a blindfold has been removed and gain instant enlightenment about your writing challenges. Even if this doesn't happen, there is still much you can use your new awareness to achieve. In Chapter 3 you will learn how to create a word self-portrait to help you:

- remove blocks
- make decisions

- address procrastination
- deal more effectively with rejection
- boost your motivation to write
- ensure that your goals are in line with who you are and that accomplishing them is truly satisfying.

What you think

By paying close attention to your thoughts, you can learn a lot that will strengthen your writing and increase your chances of success. Working on your thinking isn't just about building confidence and self-belief. Our thinking influences every aspect of our writing and there's almost always some component of your thoughts you can change to address the challenges you face and assist your ascent to becoming a more successful writer.

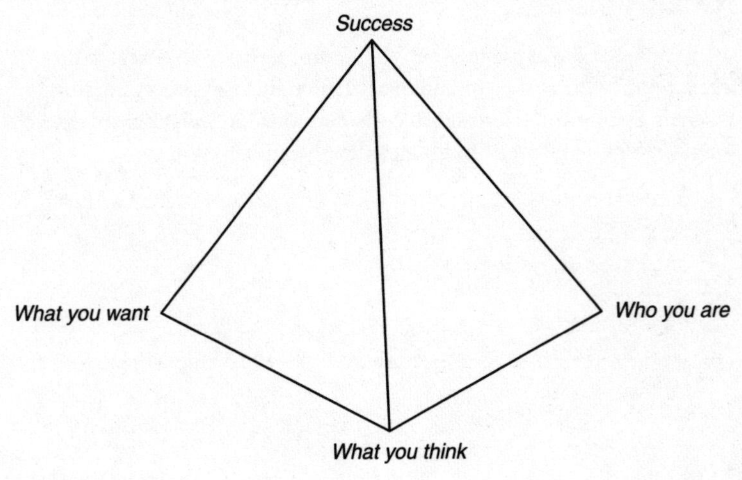

The foundations of success.

1

What do you want?

In this chapter you will learn:
- *the reasons it's important to spend time reflecting on what you want to achieve*
- *the reasons you may be chasing goals you don't want*
- *how to identify 'hidden' dreams, goals and ambitions*
- *to consider your writing in the context of your whole life.*

Why it's important to consider what you want

You may be completely sure you know what you want to achieve with your writing. However, taking a good look at the success you are chasing, both in your writing and your whole life, can have a profound effect on what you accomplish. Here's why.

REASON 1

You need to know what long-term success means to you.

Having a firm understanding of what you want to accomplish makes you less likely to:

- drift away from your goals
- lose motivation
- chase achievements you don't really want.

Insight

It can be easy to focus only on short-term success. Considering the bigger picture helps ensure we're aiming for short-term successes that build to create and support genuinely satisfying long-term success.

REASON 2

You need to spend sufficient time considering your goals.

How often do you stop to think about what you want your future to be? Although you will undoubtedly have thought about it, how much of that was quality sit-down-and-pay-full-attention time? Most people take longer planning their holidays than their lives. Taking a comprehensive look at what you really want out of life:

- helps you focus on what you know you want
- assists you to remember things you had forgotten you wanted
- allows you to find new things that excite you
- gives the success you achieve a greater chance of being genuinely fulfilling
- stops you putting off what you really want to achieve.

REASON 3

You may be asking for what you think you can have rather than what you really want.

The fact that you're reading this book shows that you're already taking the belief that you can be a writer seriously. However, echoes from your past and any negative influences around you can still have an enormous impact on your ability to be as successful as you could be. This is something you'll be able to explore further at various points in this book. In this chapter, simply use this awareness to stop any unrealistic doubts about your potential preventing you from identifying what you truly want to achieve. You will be prompted to address the reality of your capabilities later.

Real life

Gina's father had been an accountant, her mother a nurse and her brother was a doctor. Gina was highly creative, yet she left her dreams of being a writer in her childhood, because her family thought being a writer was an unrealistic way to earn a living and a waste of time. It wasn't until she was nearly 50 that Gina realized she could have a job using her creative abilities. Up until then she had been working in admin, asking for what she thought she could have, not what she wanted.

Finally Gina made the decision to take her writing seriously. Yet, she still struggled to follow the path she really desired, because the echoes from her past told her she shouldn't pursue it, writing wasn't a 'proper job' and she was wasting her time.

REASON 4

Your dreams may not be what you really want.

Coaching experience

When I asked Andrew, 'What accomplishments must you achieve to consider your life to have been satisfying and well lived?', his immediate response was, 'I don't want to be Conan Doyle or Raymond Chandler!'

This might not sound like a great answer, or even a proper answer, but for Andrew it was a thunderbolt. His father had been a detective sergeant who loved crime fiction and had written copious notes of ideas for detective novels that he planned to write when he retired. Unfortunately, he died before retiring.

Although Andrew did not believe there was a market for his father's old-fashioned ideas, he had been writing a modern crime novel for over a year, not realizing he was being driven by grief, to chase his father's dream of being a crime novelist. By stopping to consider what he really wanted, Andrew recognized he wanted to write something far more literary.

Without fully examining what he wanted to achieve, Andrew could have spent years, possibly his whole life, attempting to publish crime novels or feeling guilty that he hadn't. Perhaps Andrew would have even written some and got them published. But would they really have made him happy? Would that have been the point when he realized that wasn't what he wanted?

Andrew is just one example of someone whose dreams don't belong to them. There are many other reasons we may be longing to achieve something we don't want. The most common are that you:

- are still chasing what your parents expected you to achieve

- are chasing what you think society expects you to achieve
- are attempting to compete with friends or siblings
- have outgrown the need to achieve that dream
- don't understand the realities of the dream
- want to prove a point
- are running away from something else and this goal appears to be an escape route.

REASON 5

The rest of your life impacts on your writing and your writing impacts on the rest of your life.

However passionate you are about your writing, you are unlikely to be so single minded you don't care about anything else. Seeing your writing success in context with your whole life is essential to understanding yourself as a writer, dealing with the unique challenges you face and building firm foundations for future success.

Identifying your dreams, goals and ambitions

EXERCISE 1: OUTLINING SUCCESS

Write the title 'My Outline for Success' at the top of the left-hand side of the first double page in your contemplation journal, and your name on the right-hand side. Write your writing goals, dreams, desires and ambitions on the left-hand page. Consider all areas, styles and genres and note anything and everything you think you want to achieve.

COACHING TIP

Coaching tip

✓ When you write your outline, don't write a list. Writing haphazardly over the page stimulates your brain more effectively and stops it subconsciously prioritizing what you've written first as being most important.

Once you've written down everything you think you want to accomplish with your writing, write on the opposite page the goals, dreams, desires and ambitions you have for all the other areas of your life.

For both your writing and your life goals, ensure you don't allow yourself to censor what you write. For now, note down everything you believe you want, whether you think you can achieve it or not.

Insight

When I think I can't achieve a goal I want to accomplish, I still take it into consideration. Firstly, there may be a way I can realize it and, even if there isn't, reflecting on the reasons I want to accomplish this goal is likely to provide me with useful personal insights.

When you feel you've run out of ideas, use the following to help you dig out any goals you've missed for both writing and your life.

1 Imagine you are in the future, coming to the end of your days. Use the prompts below to write a short paragraph, or a few notes, on a fresh page of your contemplation journal about each of the following:
   - The best thing about my career was...
   - I spent my money on...
   - When I had fun I...
   - My friends were...
   - My family were...
   - The place(s) I lived...
   - I'm really proud that I...
   - The most important event of my life was...
   - My writing was...
   - As a writer I...

2 Imagine you died five minutes ago. Complete the following sentence as many times as you can:
   - I wish I had...

   Once you think you have finished, search for two more answers, or even more, if you can find them.

3 Ask yourself the following questions:
   - What do I want to achieve that I haven't achieved yet?
   - What am I putting off until I am older/the time is right/ I have more time?
   - What accomplishments must I achieve to consider my life to have been satisfying and well lived?
   - What do I want to leave behind for the people I know and love and for the rest of the world?
   - What is missing from my life?
   - What would make my life more fulfilling or more exciting?

EXERCISE 2: COMBINING YOUR GOALS WITH THE BIGGER PICTURE

Close your eyes and think about how you want your future life to be. Visualize what you will be doing ten years from now. Where will you be living? Who are your friends?

Insight

I regularly spend time visualizing my future life, creating bright, appealing images and allowing myself to feel the excitement and pleasure of living that life. As well as encouraging me to examine the future, these daydreams increase my subconscious motivation to achieve the goals I set.

Compare your outline for success with your visualization and answer the following questions:

- How do your achievements lead to your future life?
- How do your achievements influence or fit in with your day-to-day routines?
- Is there anything you need to change in your outline for success or your future visualization for them to be congruent with each other? If so, make the appropriate changes.

Reality check

Ask yourself how much your future life will cost to maintain. How are you going to fund it? How big is the gap between what you have now and what you will need in the future? If there is a gap, how are you going to bridge it? Once you've considered these questions, ask yourself if you need to modify or add to the goals on your outline for success, in order to finance your future life. If you do, make any necessary amendments.

MOVING ON

Well done! You've completed the first step towards building stronger foundations for success. Now you've got your goals out in the open, it's time to consider who you are.

10 THINGS TO REMEMBER

1. When working to achieve success as a writer, it's important to identify your dreams, goals and ambitions in your whole life as well as those that relate to your writing.
2. Having clear goals helps you to remain on course and stay motivated.
3. Spending sufficient time considering what you want to achieve means your successes should be truly satisfying.
4. Aim for what you want, not what you think you can have.
5. Always ensure your dreams are your own.
6. The rest of your life impacts on your writing and your writing impacts on the rest of your life.
7. Jot down your goals randomly on your outline for success. If you write a list, you will subconsciously prioritize them in that order.
8. When you initially identify your goals, note down whatever comes to mind without censoring what you write.
9. Visualizing the achievement of your goals helps build motivation to accomplish them.
10. When you design your future life, take into consideration how you will finance it.

2

Who do you need to be?

In this chapter you will learn:
- *to consider the labels we give ourselves*
- *to identify personal qualities and skills you need to gain or expand to achieve your writing ambitions.*

Labels

Have you ever been thought of, thought of yourself, or thought of somebody else, as 'lacking confidence'? 'A reliable person'? 'Naturally organized'? 'Always late'? 'Quiet'? 'Shy'? 'Outgoing'?

Perhaps you've had a label like this since childhood. A lot of people do, because it's easy to continue to behave the way we're expected to, especially if family and friends make comments like, 'She always was the brainy one,' or 'Peter never did like meeting new people.'

While these labels may feel permanent, in reality we don't have to conform to them unless we want to. Our labels are not who we are. They are the behaviours we have exhibited in the past, which we don't have to continue into the future. We can choose to change, both the identities others impose on us and the way we expect ourselves to behave.

ONGOING EXERCISE

Ongoing exercise – checking for labels

In the future, make a conscious effort to notice when people label you or expect you to behave in a certain way. Each time you notice this happen, consider if you're happy to continue conforming to these expectations or if you need or want to change.

Choosing to change

Although we often conform to the identities we acquire, we also inevitably change in other ways. Life experiences, such as leaving school, starting work, serious illness or having children change us. So, if the idea you can choose to change on purpose feels odd or unattainable, remember:

- You change as you move through life, but these changes are rarely consciously acknowledged.
- Choosing to change doesn't mean pretending to be someone you aren't. It means genuinely developing a skill or behaviour.
- It's usually far more productive to change on purpose than by reacting to the buffeting and random lessons life teaches us.
- Identifying the personal qualities and behaviours you need to have to achieve your goals then working to build them (rather than recognizing after the event that you would have been better off having them) will increase the odds of accomplishing your goals and shorten the time it takes to realize your ambitions.

I am the type of person content to spend hours on my own in front of the computer. Once I became published, I was expected to be not only a public speaker, but a stand-up comedian.

Candy Gourlay – children's author

Insight

Choosing to change is the same as taking action to improve your writing skills to produce better prose. To be a successful writer you need to have the right personal qualities as well as strong writing skills.

Identifying changes you need to make

For the remainder of this chapter you will only be asked to consider your writing goals. However, the techniques found here can be applied to the rest of your life if you wish.

EXERCISE 1: WHO DO YOU NEED TO BE TO ACHIEVE YOUR GOALS?

Consider the outline for success you created in Chapter 1. For each writing achievement you have identified, ask yourself:

- What sort of person achieves this?

- What are the personal qualities or behaviours that will assist them to accomplish it?

As you ask these questions of each achievement, make a list of everything you identify in your contemplation journal.

Coaching experience

Sophie was studying an MA in Screenwriting. She listed the following qualities as the ones she either believed a successful scriptwriter needed or had seen successful professional scriptwriters display:

Confidence	Humour	Energy
Focus	Compassion	Conviction
Creativity	Observation	Honesty
Imagination	Detachment	Integrity
Unlimited ideas	Bravery	Commitment
Generosity	Motivation	Bravery
Kindness	Self-promotion	Heart and soul
Concentration	Charm	Thick-skinned
Discipline	Likeability	Shallow
Inspiration	Charisma	Manipulative
Sensitivity	Positivity	Pushiness
Passion	Enthusiasm	Scheming
Intelligence	Strength	Boastful
Wit	Determination	Selfish

EXERCISE 2: DO YOU NEED TO SHED YOUR SKIN?

Consider the qualities you have identified in Exercise 1. Score on a scale of 1 to 10 how much you think you already have each quality. (10 = I have this quality in abundance, 1 = I don't believe I have this quality at all.)

For any quality that scores less than seven, consider if it is something you want to take on board or if you want to increase your score for having this quality. If it is, write increasing or gaining that quality as a goal on your outline for success at the front of your contemplation journal.

Qualities you don't want

You may find there are some qualities or behaviours on your list that you do not want to develop as you consider them undesirable or they confront your integrity.

Coaching experience

Sophie had noted that she sometimes considered successful scriptwriters were:

Thick-skinned
Shallow
Manipulative
Pushy
Scheming
Boastful
Selfish

She didn't want to be a person who behaved like this at any time and also recognized that these qualities had their down sides. For example, she said becoming more thick-skinned would 'erode her relationships' – both professional and personal – and would 'reduce the sensitivity a writer needs to produce quality writing'.

Sophie chose not to add these behaviours to her outline for success. However, she recognized that sometimes there was an advantage for scriptwriters who acted in these ways. She therefore considered what the benefits were.

Some of the qualities Sophie didn't want were simply an extreme of skills she had already recognized as being important to support her success. For example, she saw being pushy as taking confidence to an undesirable level.

Sophie's reflection led her to create new goals to incorporate the benefits she saw. For example, she set the goal, 'I am able to maintain confidence and creativity when I receive negative criticism or rejection.' This acknowledged her recognition that being thick-skinned could be helpful under some circumstances.

If you identified undesirable behaviours in Exercise 1, remove them, or word a new goal to bring what you really want.

Reality check

Are you comfortable with the idea of taking on or building the qualities and behaviours you have identified? If you're not, consider what alternatives might help you achieve the same result. If you really don't feel comfortable with the idea of having one or more of the attributes you consider essential to succeeding, reflect on whether the goals you have identified are really what you want.

Standing up in front of a large number of people fills me with dread! If I wasn't a writer, I wouldn't have to do it, but to sell my books, I've had to learn to accept this and to do it. It scares me witless! But, when you write full time, you have to change your behaviour in order to survive.

Simon Whaley – author and freelance writer

MOVING ON

Don't worry at this stage if you don't know how to make the changes you need to make, or even if you don't believe you can make them. You've just been looking into the future and identifying your ideals. You will work on manifesting the realities in later chapters. But before you consider that, come back to the present and consider who you are today. After all, the only place we can start making changes is where we are right now.

10 THINGS TO REMEMBER

1. People label you as who they think you are, but you don't have to conform to these labels.
2. You inevitably change as you move through life.
3. You can choose to change who you are.
4. Changing who you are is not about being disingenuous – it is about becoming someone you want to be.
5. It can feel odd adopting new behaviours, but change is a completely natural.
6. Changing on purpose allows you to improve your skills to become a more successful writer.
7. You are more likely to get what you want if you become the sort of person who achieves that goal.
8. Make sure the qualities you identify as necessary to achieve your goals don't undermine ones you already have that are just as necessary.
9. Don't adopt behaviours that contradict the person you want to be because you think successful writers behave that way. You won't achieve true happiness and fulfilment unless you stay true to your own morals and values.
10. Identifying who you need to be to achieve a particular goal may lead to you discarding or reframing that goal.

3

Who are you?

In this chapter you will learn:

- ***how to develop a clearer understanding of what drives your motivation***
- ***how to identify and prioritize your core values.***

Core values

Our core values are fundamental principles that are important to us. They have a strong pull on our emotions and desires and therefore influence our decisions, focus, motivation, confidence, our reaction to rejection, what stresses us and ultimately what we achieve. They are identified by simple descriptors such as respect, honesty, support, fun, creativity, individuality, security…

By defining ourselves in a simple word-portrait of our core values we can:

- ▶ understand our motivation and loss of motivation
- ▶ build greater motivation to accomplish our ambitions
- ▶ recognize why we sometimes act against achieving what we think we want to achieve
- ▶ understand the causes of some of the challenges we experience.

Coaching experience

Tim was a scriptwriter. Although he loved writing, he realized he had become resistant to finishing anything. He would constantly create excuses and diversions to stop himself completing a script until the very last moment. A couple of times he had even overrun deadlines. The quality of his work was deteriorating along with his reputation.

While reflecting on this situation, Tim recognized that he was happy when he was writing, but discontented once others became involved. He acknowledged that this was because others began to add their interpretations and ideas. He realized he was holding back on finishing scripts, or even treatments, because it held off the moment others began 'interfering' with his ideas.

Eliciting Tim's core values helped him identify that they included appreciation, respect and independence.

Recognizing that he had a strong value of independence allowed Tim to understand why he was reacting so emotionally when he felt as if people were 'interfering'. He also recognized that when he was working with people who showed a lack of respect or appreciation for his work, he was reacting even more strongly, because respect and appreciation were also two of his core values.

Once Tim understood why he was behaving the way he was, he chose to remind himself of the good things about being a scriptwriter. The key positives were that scriptwriting allowed him to earn his living by being creative and most days it gave him the freedom to structure his day how he wanted to. Tim also reminded himself that the other people's 'interfering' was helping bring his script to life and he couldn't do that without them. He still had to grit his teeth occasionally. However, now he knew why he behaved the way he did, Tim could stop himself reacting automatically when he perceived he was experiencing loss of independence, disrespect or lack of appreciation. This reduced the negative emotion he felt and Tim became motivated to see his scripts through to completion again.

Tim also decided to be more discriminating about whom he worked with in the future. This enabled him to receive greater respect and appreciation. Finally, he made longer-term plans to become a writer–director, so that he would have greater autonomy over his writing.

Your core values

The following exercises will take you through a process to identify your core values, their order of importance and what they mean to you.

EXERCISE 1: TAKE A LOOK AT YOUR LIFE

Make a list of answers in your contemplation journal as you do the following – single words or a short sentence for each response will be most helpful:

- Look around your home and, for each room, ask, 'What does this room tell me is important to me?' Keep asking the question until you can find no more answers and then move on to the next room. If you get the same answer(s) in more than one room, only note them down once.
- Look through the belongings that are totally yours: your handbag, wardrobe, bookshelf, drawers, pockets. Anywhere you alone put stuff. What do these things tell you is important to you? Add these to your list unless they are already there.
- Identify the activities you choose to spend your free time on and add them to your list. Also add the activities you would like to spend your free time on, but are currently unable to.
- Note down the places you choose to go regularly and the places you have really enjoyed being.
- Write down who you enjoy spending time with, and write down separately what you value most about your relationship with them.
- Name five people you admire – whether you know them or not, whether they are real or fictional.
- Think about the times you've experienced when things were going really well; when you were in the flow and fully energized by what was happening. Add these to your list.
- Also add to your list times when you have felt truly happy.

Example
Here is part of the list aspiring novelist Kate created in response to Exercise 1:

Cats
Books
Humour
Writing
Tennis
Reading
Dancing
Family
My son
I value my son's sense of humour and his considerate nature.
The birth of my son.

Insight

Even something as simple as our favourite animal can reflect deep aspects of our personality.

EXERCISE 2: IDENTIFYING YOUR CORE VALUES

At first glance this exercise may seem a little complex. However, it's really quite a simple process. If you read through from here until you reach the start of Exercise 3, before you start working on Exercise 2, what you need to do should be quite clear.

Consider the list you created in Exercise 1. For the first answer on the list, ask yourself, 'What's important to me about this?' Make a note of your answer(s), then ask the same question again of that/those answer(s). Keep asking 'What's important to me about this?' of each answer you get, until you keep coming up with the same answer. Write this final answer in your contemplation journal – this is one of your core values.

Notes

- If asking 'What's important to me about this?' seems to be an odd question to ask of a particular item on your list, instead ask, 'What do I like about this?'
- Some of the words on your list from Exercise 1 may already be values. Therefore you will only need to ask once, 'What's important to me about this?' before you get to the root of what's important to you about them. Other concepts on the list will require you to ask the question a lot more times.

Example
When Kate considered what was important/what she liked about cats, she came up with the answers:

They're independent.
They're clever.

To the question, 'What's important about being independent?' Kate answered:

Being independent.

Independence is therefore one of Kate's core values.

To the question, 'What's important about being clever?' Kate answered:

You can see solutions other people can't.
You can get yourself out of difficult situations.

To the question, 'What's important about seeing solutions other people can't?' Kate answered:

You come up with exciting new ideas.

To the question, 'What's important about new ideas?' Kate answered:

They're an expression of creativity.
No one has thought of them before.

To the question, 'What's important about expressing creativity?' Kate answered:

Creativity.

Creativity is therefore one of Kate's core values.

Note
In the example given:

- Kate would also need to ask, 'What's important about being able to get yourself out of difficult situations?' and 'What's important about no one having thought of something before?' She would need to explore the answers those questions generated in the same way.
- Kate used the word 'exciting' to describe ideas. This is purely an expression of the way she feels. If Kate had said 'fun new ideas' then she should also have considered what was important about the ideas being fun.

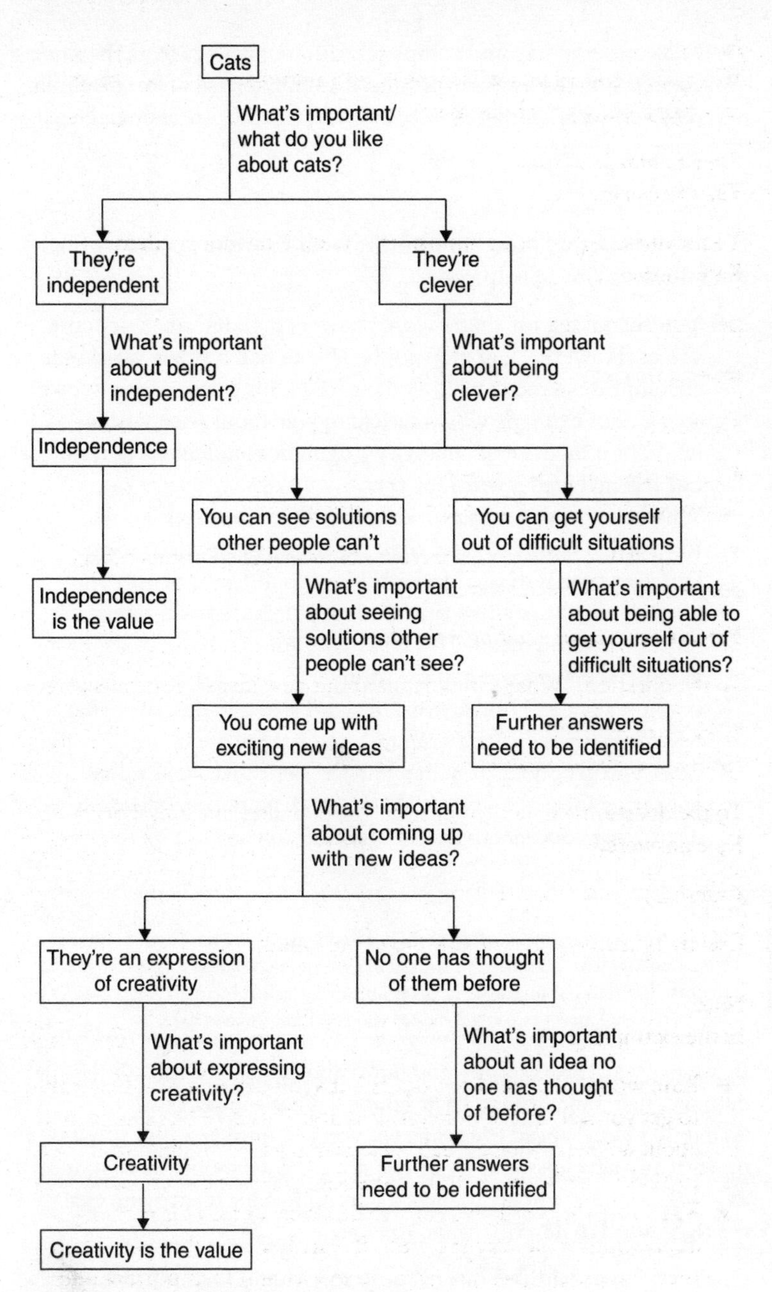

Figure 3.1 Identifying values from what is important to you.

- ▶ Someone else may find completely different values from the same concepts on the list Kate produced from Exercise 1. For example, they may see what they like about cats is that they are agile and regal.

COACHING TIPS

Coaching tips

Before you start working on your list from Exercise 1, read through the following tips to help you.

- ✓ You're looking for single-word answers that describe your core values. However, you may not be able to find a single word that encompasses exactly what you mean. In this case create a 'word string'. For example what matters to you about your writing might be a mixture of creativity/originality/uniqueness that no one has invented a word for yet.
- ✓ When you do this exercise remember it is about you. Look for word(s) that really feel right for what you are describing. Different words mean different things to different people and it's well worth spending time finding words that accurately reflect what you mean. This will make your core values list more helpful when you use it in the future.
- ✓ If you really can't find a word or word string to describe what you mean, then create a brief note to encapsulate it.
- ✓ Once you get going, you may find the same ideas and values appearing more than once. This is good. It confirms that you are identifying concepts that are important to you.

Insight

In my experience, some clients are able to break every answer down to 'love', believing that love is at the very root of everything that matters. If this is the case for you, put love as your most important value, but also list as core values the final answers you get before you reach the answer love.

If, having read the examples and notes above, you are still a little daunted, just remember to keep asking, 'What's important?' or 'What do I like?' about every answer you get, until you don't come up with any new answers. Once you get going, it should be easy and, as a writer, you are likely to have a natural feel for identifying exactly the right word to describe what you mean.

Once you have identified one or more core values that underpin the first item on your list from Exercise 1, move on to the next item.

Work on it in the same way as before. Continue to work through the list from Exercise 1 until you have considered everything on it.

This exercise may take quite a while depending on what you come up with. If you don't have time to work all in one go on all the items on your list from Exercise 1, stop when you run out of time and come back later. You will lose nothing by working on each item at separate intervals, but if you rush to get through the list you might miss something important.

EXERCISE 3: CORE VALUES FROM NEGATIVES

Once more it's worth reading to the end of this exercise before you start to work on it.

Create a list of:

- anyone you have a bad relationship with, or who upsets you, or who makes you mad
- anything that makes you cross
- anything you particularly don't like (don't include any food)
- any situations that make you feel uncomfortable.

Think back to the last time you were cross or even angry. What happened that made you mad? What were the reasons you got angry? Add this/these to your list.

Once you have your list, take one item at a time and dig for the root cause of the aggravation in the same way you dug for values in Exercise 2 above. However, this time keep asking yourself questions such as 'Why does this make me cross?', 'What don't I like about this?', 'What are the reasons why this stresses me?' Keep asking the same question of an item until you keep coming up with an answer that identifies a value that is being confronted, offended or taken away from you.

Coaching experience

Everyone at work liked Ling's boss, even Ling. But there were times when he made her cross. She particularly disliked the way he sometimes expected her to stay late, even if it was only for five minutes. She also hated it when he perched on the corner of her desk to talk to her. Furthermore, she became annoyed when he parked his four-wheel drive in the space she liked to park in.

(Contd)

When I asked Ling what the reasons were that she got so cross with her boss for making her stay just five minutes late, she realized that she didn't usually mind. She only got cross when he asked her to stay late to do a job he could have asked her to do earlier. She said this was because he should be more organized. I asked what the reasons were that she thought he should be more organized. Ling said, 'organization is important'. When I asked her why organization was important, she told me again that organization was important.

Ling also considered why she hated her boss sitting on the corner of her desk. She recognized it was because he moved things to make space to sit on. When I asked the reasons she didn't like him moving things, she said, 'I like to be organized'. When I enquired further, she told me once more, 'organization is important'.

Finally I asked Ling why she felt her boss shouldn't park in a parking space that didn't belong to anyone in particular. She said she liked to park in the same place every day and everyone knew that except her boss. When I asked her what was important about parking in the same space she said, 'I like order'. She smiled and said, 'organization and order are very important to me.'

These observations led Ling to recognize that she thought it important to be organized and orderly. She considered then the same concept and therefore termed this value organization/order.

Beware

When you look at your dislikes and situations where you feel uncomfortable, remember that some of your feelings may be generated by fear or lack self-confidence or self-belief. For example, you may feel uncomfortable in a large crowd of strangers. This may be because you value peace and quiet, but it may also be because you lack confidence to hold conversations with new people, feel claustrophobic, have experience of a crowd acting violently, fear having your wallet stolen, or one of many other possibilities. Lacking confidence or fear are basic human responses and are unlikely to be linked to any values.

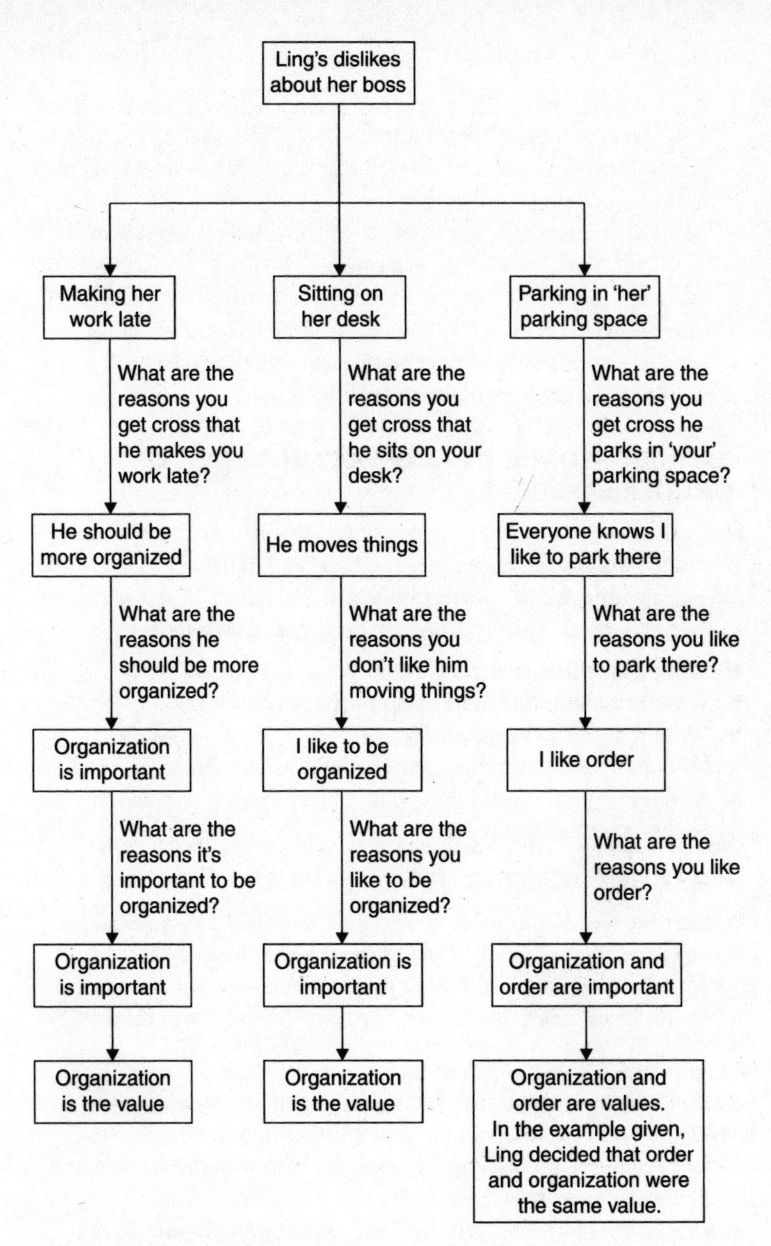

Figure 3.2 Identifying values from negatives.

Coaching tips

- ✓ A good question to ask, if you're unsure whether a negative is linked to a value, is 'What do I fear here?' This should enable you to identify if you fear something on a basic survival level or if a value is being confronted.
- ✓ Be aware that certain stressors are universal. For example most people don't enjoy waiting in a queue. You are likely to chase this back to the fact that the queue is preventing you spending time elsewhere. However that's unlikely to tell you anything new, just you'd rather be spending time on other activities, fulfilling whatever values they are linked to.

EXERCISE 4: ONCE YOU HAVE A COMPLETE LIST OF CORE VALUES

Have a final check of the words you have identified as core values. Core values are the basic qualities we gain or experience. Things such as money, your cat, fast cars or family are not values. If you're stuck or unsure if something is a value, see if it breaks down by asking:

- ▶ What does this give me?
- ▶ What is it about this that makes me happy?
- ▶ What reasons do I need this?
- ▶ If I didn't have this in my life, what would be missing?
- ▶ Also remember, if something is an object, person or group of people it isn't a core value.

EXERCISE 5: SORTING OUT YOUR VALUES

Consider the words and word strings you identified as your final list of core values. Ask yourself if any of them mean the same thing to you. If they do, use the word that means the most to you and remove the other one, or create a word string to express what you mean.

Examples

- ▶ You may have the words 'recognition' and 'acknowledgement' as two separate core values. When you reflect you may realize they mean the same thing and replace them with the word string 'recognition/acknowledgement'.
- ▶ Or you may have 'recognition' and 'acknowledgement' as two separate core values. When you reflect, you may realize that it's the recognition that acknowledgement brings which excites you. You therefore need to remove 'acknowledgement' from your list.

▶ Or you may see 'recognition' and 'acknowledgement' as separate concepts and have them both on your list.

Insight

The same words may arouse different ideas and feelings in different people. What matters is that you are satisfied that all your core values are separate concepts and you are comfortable with the words you use to describe them.

EXERCISE 6: MISSING WORDS

Spend a little time reflecting on the values you have identified and ask yourself, 'Are there any more core values I hold?' Also be open to recognising your core values as you go about your life. When things excite you, are pleasurable or make you cross, mentally check your values list to identify which buttons are being pressed, then ask, 'Is there something else about this that is important?' This will not only help you find values you might have missed, but will help you find personal benefits from your core values. For example we usually get angry when someone confronts or negates one of our core values. Understanding that we are getting angry because a particular value is being confronted can help reduce the stress and anger that situation would otherwise create.

Coaching tip

COACHING TIP

✓ Don't 'go shopping' for values you feel you ought to have. Just because a value isn't on your list, it doesn't mean you don't think it matters, it's just not as high a priority as others.

Coaching experience

Children's writer Cassie was initially concerned that she hadn't identified truth as one of her personal values. Since she saw herself as truthful person, she added it to her self-portrait. However, once she began working with her personal values, she recognized there were times when she was happy to hold back from telling the truth, for example, when she didn't want to hurt other people's feelings.

EXERCISE 7: PUTTING YOUR VALUES IN PRIORITY ORDER

Once more it's worth reading to the end of this exercise before you start to work on it.

Take the list of core values you have just created. Compare the top value with the next value on your list. Pretend you have to live without one of them – which one would you give up most easily? Asking this question allows you to identify which value is most important out of the two.

Example

Let's say your list contains the following:

- Respect
- Understanding/learning
- Recognition
- Adventure
- Peace/calm
- Expression/creativity/inspiration
- Caring
- Integrity

First compare 'respect' with 'understanding/learning' and ask yourself which one you would give up most easily. If you believe you would give up respect before understanding/learning then understanding/learning is the more important of the two.

Note

It can be difficult to choose between your values, because you are comparing concepts that are all of great importance to you.

Once you have decided which value is most important, put a mark next to it and then pair the top value with the third value on the list. Move on through the list comparing the top value with everything else on the entire list.

Example

For the list above you would first pair respect with understanding/ learning, then respect with recognition, then respect with adventure, then respect with peace/calm, and so on, each time putting a mark against the value that is most important, until you have compared respect with every other word on the list.

Note
When you have done this, your list will have several marks against your values. The marks could all be against the first value – if it is your most important value – or against some words and not others, in any amounts, scattered against the words on the list.

Once you have considered the first value on the list, compare the second value with all the values below it, one at a time.

Example
For the list above you would now compare understanding/learning with recognition, then understanding/learning with adventure, then understanding/learning with peace/calm and so on, each time putting a mark against the value that is most important, until you have compared understanding/learning with every other word on the list.

Note
In this example you do not compare understanding/learning with respect, because you have already made that comparison.

When you have considered the second word against all the values below it, compare the third word with all the values below that. Work your way through the whole list in this manner until you have compared each word with every other word once.

Beware
Don't give priority to a value because you think it ought to have a higher priority. Go for what you really feel.

You should end up with a list that looks something like this, but will of course contain your own core values:

Respect	IIIIIII
Understanding/learning	IIII
Recognition	I
Adventure	IIIIII
Peace/calm	
Expression/creativity/inspiration	IIIII
Caring	II
Integrity	III

COACHING TIPS

Coaching tips

- ✓ It may help to have someone else read out your values in pairs.
- ✓ If you're having trouble deciding between your values, the following exercise can help you separate them:
  - ▷ Imagine you are being chased by a pack of wolves. You know you can't outrun them. Your only hope is to cross the river ahead, which is too wide and too deep for them to follow. But there is only an old weatherworn rowing boat to take you to the opposite riverbank. The boat is so fragile it can only hold you and one of your core values. Anything you leave behind will be torn to shreds by the wolves.
  - ▷ Taking your values two at a time, decide which one you will leave behind and which one you will take across the river with you. Repeat this scenario as many times as you need, so you have compared all your values with each other, one at a time.
  - ▷ When you have finished comparing your values, add up the score for each one to identify their order of importance to you.

EXERCISE 8: NOTING DOWN YOUR CORE VALUES

List your core values in priority order in your achievement log. Put the highest scoring first. If any have the same score, ask yourself again which is most important, and put the most important above the other one.

Note

If you have identified more than 12 core values, decide where there seems to be a natural divide of importance somewhere between your sixth and twelfth ranked values. Write only the top six to 12 values in your achievement log.

EXERCISE 9: EXPLORING YOUR VALUES

Consider the values you have written in your achievement log one at a time. Write an explanation of your understanding of each value. Write three to four sentences at least, but if you want to write more, write as much as you want to.

Coaching experience

Here are some examples of core value descriptions written by my clients:

RELIABILITY

'I like to be able to count on others and hope that they can rely on me. I think that loyalty and respect link together on this. They are not all part of one value, but they complement each other and work together to strengthen the whole of who I am.'

UNIQUENESS/INDIVIDUALITY

'I totally seek to be an individual and always love the individuality of my friends. I love that they are unique and there is no one quite like them. Indeed we are all unique and therefore fascinating and intriguing, but many people fail to celebrate this by attempting to conform to others' ideals. This saddens me. I love the differences in everything.'

FUN/LAUGHTER

'Nothing lifts me, cheers me, energizes me more than a good laugh and having fun with friends and family. I think even in times of great sadness there is always humour, and humour gets you through. I want this to be seen in my writing too.'

Insight

You may wish to explore your thoughts in your contemplation journal, before giving a more concise definition of each value in your achievement log.

Well done! You have now identified your core values. However, don't worry if the list doesn't seem quite right. Your true list of core values may take some time to compile and may need to rest and be revisited before it is acceptable to you. Also remember that values can change over time and therefore need to be revisited about once a year. Even if they haven't changed, it's important to spend time reminding yourself of them and what they mean to you.

EXERCISE 10: MISSED ANY GOALS?

Return to your outline for success. Are there any further dreams, goals or ambitions that thinking about who you are has brought to mind? Is there anything to add, change or even remove? Also reconsider the bigger picture you visualized. Anything you want to change here? If so, make the necessary changes.

MOVING ON

About 90 per cent of my clients are surprised by the impact unearthing their core values has on them and their writing. If you're not feeling that way (or even slightly that way) don't worry, that's exactly how I felt the first time I clarified my core values. Nevertheless, since then, I have been amazed at the insights they have given me. I've also witnessed them bring life-changing understanding to hundreds of other people.

Whatever you feel right now, take time to note how your values connect to the way you feel and the way you react at times of excitement, confusion or stress in the future. That way your appreciation of them should grow and grow.

In the next chapter you'll be shown how to use your core values to set more satisfying goals, and later on in this book you can discover how to use core values to overcome some of your writing challenges.

10 THINGS TO REMEMBER

1. Your core values are fundamental principles or essential qualities that are important to you.
2. Core values have a strong influence on your emotions and desires and therefore ultimately on what you achieve.
3. Core values are identified by simple descriptors such as respect, honesty, support, fun, creativity, individuality, security…
4. If you can't find a single word to describe a core value, create a 'word string' or a brief note to encapsulate what you mean.
5. If something is an object, person or group of people it isn't a core value.
6. Most characteristics are both a strength and a weakness, it's how you use them that matters.
7. Don't 'go shopping' for core values that you feel you ought to have.
8. Your true list of core values may take some time to compile and may need to rest and be revisited before it is acceptable to you.
9. Values can change over time.
10. Revisit your core values once a year – or more often if you wish. Even if they haven't changed, it's important to spend time reminding yourself of them and what they mean to you.

4

Linking who you are to what you want to achieve

In this chapter you will learn:

- ***how your goals and core values fit together***
- ***to explore the realities of your writing goals***
- ***more about why you want to be a writer (or perhaps why you don't)***
- ***to identify your priorities.***

What do you really want?

Chapter 1 discussed how the influence of external expectations, or getting caught up in others' dreams, can lead us to strive for false goals. Just like Andrew in Chapter 1, who spent years thinking he wanted to write a crime novel, we may think we want something, but we don't. We start travelling down a road and become so focused on our goal that we forget to look up. Maybe we didn't really want the goal in the first place, or maybe we've changed or our life has changed. But still we continue, because we're so focused on the goal. Finally we reach our destination, only to discover we don't want to be there. Chapter 4 aims to help you check that what you've identified in Chapters 1 and 2 really is what you want before you chase off after it.

EXERCISE 1: LINKING GOALS TO VALUES

Consider in turn each goal you identified in your outline for success. For each one, ask yourself which of your core values it satisfies. Make a note of this in your contemplation journal.

Note

Each goal is likely to satisfy more than one core value.

- If you find any goals that don't satisfy at least one core value, ask yourself if this goal facilitates another goal that does.
- If it does, make a note of this in your contemplation journal.
- If it doesn't, use your contemplation journal to ask yourself the following questions:
  - Is this a goal I want to achieve or is it someone else's dream?
  - Am I chasing this goal because I believe it will take me away from someone, something or some situation I don't like?
  - Is this goal something someone else expects of me? If it is, ask, 'What are my reasons for living up to this expectation?'
  - How will achieving this goal add to my life?
  - How will not achieving this goal detract from my life?
  - Is this a past aim that is no longer congruent with who I am today or who I want to be in the future?
  - Have I been convinced I want to work on this goal because it suits someone else for me to achieve it?
  - Is this goal truly what I want?

Having considered these questions, ask yourself, 'Do I still want to keep this goal in my outline for success?'

Make any changes necessary to your outline.

Insight

If a goal does not satisfy at least one core value, we are unlikely to find sufficient motivation to achieve it and if we do, we are unlikely to find it genuinely fulfilling.

EXERCISE 2: REFLECTING ON YOUR WRITING GOALS

Ask yourself the following questions:

- What values do my writing goals satisfy? (Different writing goals may satisfy different values.)
- What values does being a writer satisfy?
- What influence do my values have specifically over the way I write and the content of what I write?
- Are all my writing goals congruent with my values?

Reflect on your answers to the questions above to ensure that your writing goals are what you really want to achieve and that they will be truly rewarding when you accomplish them. This reflection may take some time, especially if it makes you question what you want to write, or even if you want to write.

Allow yourself all the time you need to explore and become sure of your true desires, and to make any appropriate changes to your outline for success. Even if this means revisiting the work you did in Chapters 1 and 2, the effort will be worth it in the long term. However, you may not need to do this at all if your reflection simply confirms that you are already pursuing goals that are congruent with who you are.

EXERCISE 3: LINKING YOUR VALUES TO YOUR FUTURE VISION

Review the visualization of your future life that you created in Chapter 1, Exercise 2. Is this congruent with your values? Do you need to change or modify anything? If so, do.

EXERCISE 4: DETERMINING PRIORITIES

Consider the importance of achieving each of the goals you have identified in your outline for success – both your writing and non-writing goals. Assign a number to each goal to denote how important it is to achieve it in relation to all the others.

Note
If you find yourself unable to decide if one goal has priority over another, assign them both the same number. It's absolutely fine for two (or more) goals to have equal priority.

Once you have decided on your priorities, you will be able to recognize how important your writing is in relation to the other goals you want to achieve. You may even find your writing isn't as important as you thought it was. If you are surprised by the prioritization of any of your goals, take out your contemplation journal and discuss what this means to you. Again, these thoughts may prompt you to modify your outline for success.

EXERCISE 5: SUCCESS

Write the answers to the following questions in your contemplation journal:

- What is success?

- What does being a successful writer mean to me? (Or 'What does being a more successful writer mean to me?' if you already consider yourself successful.)
- What activities will being a successful writer include?

Write down a definition in your achievement log that will enable you to identify when you become a successful writer. Keeping this definition firmly in focus, use your contemplation journal to answer the following questions:

- What will I gain by becoming a (more) successful writer?
- What will I lose by becoming a (more) successful writer?
- How will becoming a (more) successful writer affect the other people in my life?
- What life consequences will becoming a (more) successful writer bring?
- Will becoming a (more) successful writer be something that truly satisfies me?

> ***Being self-employed is tough and writing is the hardest job I've ever had. It's also far and away the most rewarding.***
>
> Della Galton – author and freelance writer

EXERCISE 6: CONSEQUENCES

If you recognise in Exercise 5 that becoming a (more) successful writer may have negative repercussions in your life, use your contemplation journal to consider:

- What actions you can take now, or in the future, to remove or reduce these repercussions?
- Are you happy with the impact you expect these repercussions to have on your life and those around you? If you aren't, are you prepared to deal with the fallout?

When you've considered your answers to these questions, remove or modify any goals whose potential impact you're unhappy with to ensure that the future consequences of your actions will be acceptable to you.

Priorities

Chances are you started reading this book because writing is one of your highest priorities. Having explored your future desires and motivation it probably still is. However, you may have discovered it isn't as important as you thought it was. You may even have decided you don't want to be a writer any more. If this is the case, and you've put a lot of time and effort into your writing goals, you may find this disheartening or even heartbreaking. If you feel this way, consider what you have learned from working on your writing. Also remember, there's no point wasting time and effort in the future on what you don't really want. Congratulate yourself on your insight, appreciate what you've learned and look forward to spending more time on what you really want to achieve.

MOVING ON

If you still want be a writer, move on to Chapter 5 to create your roadmap to success.

10 THINGS TO REMEMBER

1. Always make sure you truly want to achieve the goals you are aiming for.
2. If a goal does not satisfy at least one core value, you are unlikely to find sufficient motivation to achieve it.
3. If you do achieve a goal that doesn't satisfy at least one core value, you are unlikely to find that achievement genuinely fulfilling.
4. Sometimes you need to achieve goals that don't satisfy any of your values in order to achieve a bigger goal that does.
5. Goals can have equal priorities.
6. Achieving your goals will impact on other people and other areas of your life.
7. You can't anticipate all the consequences of achieving your goals, but it's important to anticipate those you can and ensure that they are acceptable to you.
8. Your writing may not be as important to you as you originally thought.
9. There's no point wasting time and effort on what you don't really want.
10. Don't be disheartened if you realize you don't want to be a writer. Appreciate what you've learned and celebrate that you've made a discovery that will save you wasting any more time on a dream you don't want.

Creating your roadmap for success

In this chapter you will learn:

- ***to create an overview for achieving all your writing goals***
- ***to outline what you want to achieve in the next twelve months***
- ***to create an action plan for what you want to achieve in the next three months.***

By creating your outline for success you've produced a cauldron of wishes bubbling away, but with no plan or structure for how you're going to get them. This chapter is going to help you transform this brew into your roadmap to success; a roadmap to help you navigate from here to the future with added octane in your engine.

Focus

Writers who succeed are the writers who focus on their priorities, and with only a few exceptions, stick to them. However, as creative people, writers have active minds that spot diversions and opportunities that encourage them to become involved elsewhere.

The trick of focusing in the face of distractions that seem more appealing is to maintain sufficient focus to succeed, while also maintaining your freedom to explore, innovate and take on new opportunities that arise. The roadmap to success is a key tool in helping achieve this; providing you with an anchor when needed, but not a straightjacket for your creativity.

USING THIS CHAPTER

If you know which direction you want to take your writing in, start with Exercise 1. If you're not sure which direction you wish to take your writing in, start at Exercise 4.

Creating your roadmap

EXERCISE 1: YOUR WRITING SUCCESS

Make a list in your achievement log of all the writing goals and writing-related goals that you have named in your outline for success. Estimate for each, how long you think it will take you to achieve it.

- For the writing goals you estimate will take less than five years to achieve, write the year of achievement beside them.
- Write '5+' beside each writing goal you expect to take between five and ten years to achieve.
- For those writing goals you expect to take between ten and 15 years, write '10+'.
- For those writing goals you expect to take between 15 and 20 years, write 15+.
- For those writing goals you expect to take more than 20 years, write 20+.

Note

You may not have identified goals you wish to achieve as far ahead as 20 years time, or even 15 or ten. This doesn't matter. Just label the goals appropriately, as far ahead as you have considered.

Coaching tip

- ✓ Don't get too hung up on timescales when you consider achieving your goals. Nothing is certain when others' approval and opinion is involved (which is so often the case with writing). Simply give a rough estimate of when you think you would like to and could realistically achieve each goal.

If you only have one or two writing goals

Perhaps you only want to write one book or want to focus on publishing articles. If this is the case then you may not need to write out a plan at this stage. But do keep it in mind if your ambitions grow.

And do remember that writing goals include activities that support your writing ambitions, such as reading sufficient books to understand your market or becoming a more confident speaker in order to give author talks when you are published. However, if you really do currently have only one or two writing goals, move to Exercise 4 and work from there, applying the exercises to your goals as closely as possible.

EXERCISE 2: CONSTRUCTING YOUR ROADMAP

Draw a table in your achievement log to illustrate the time estimates you established in Exercise 1. For an example of how to do this, see Figure 5.1 which is a time plan for a fictitious would-be comedy writer called Jack. Jack intends to use stand-up to promote and enhance his writing career.

Notes

Jack's overview is for a career that reaches the upper echelons of being a professional comedian. You may well have many fewer goals if your plans are not so ambitious.

Jack may never achieve his highest goals, but if they are what he truly desires, his plans need to have the potential to lead him there.

COACHING TIPS

Coaching tips

- ✓ You will notice Jack's goals are mostly ill defined. Jack doesn't specify which comedy writing course he is taking, which books to read, or how much to save each year. That sort of detail isn't important for now – we'll come back to details later.
- ✓ Don't get too tied up with timescales or having every goal you need in the plan. The important thing is to get down some form of structure about where you are headed. You can fill in the gaps as you go along and no doubt you will find other paths to follow in the future. Your timescales for achieving some goals will undoubtedly change and later on you may also want to remove goals you realize you no longer want or need. For example, perhaps Jack will discover he doesn't like publicity very much and curtail the stand-up activities. Or perhaps he will like stand-up so much he will give up the dreams of writing an acclaimed TV comedy show.

Year 1	Year 2	Year 3	Year 4	Year 5	By year 10	By year 15	By year 20
Take comedy writers' course	Take stand-up classes	Take scriptwriting classes	Have local fan-base	Perform at the Edinburgh fringe	National fan base	Have own TV sketch show	Have best-selling biography
Attend public speaking course	Have friends who are comedy writers	Perform stand-up in local pubs	Perform in comedy clubs	Collaborate with other comedy writers	Teaching stand-up and/or comedy writing	Have own TV stand-up show	Host game shows
Read six 'how to' books on writing comedy	Write my own stand-up material	Build my own website	Sketches used by stage/radio sketch show	Go down to working part time in 'day job'	UK stand-up tour	Have written highly acclaimed TV comedy show	Celebrity guest on TV chat shows/ quiz show
Start savings fund to support writing				Have strong networking connections			

Figure 5.1 Jack's overview.

- ✓ Unexpected things happen in life, holding you up, speeding you on, changing your perspective and direction. None of this matters at this stage. All you need to do is write down:
  - ▷ Your current writing goals.
  - ▷ Goals that support or enhance your current writing goals.
  - ▷ A rough timescale of when you'll achieve these goals.
  - ▷ Some understanding of how your goals fit together.
- ✓ You will notice that Jack has stated each goal only once in his overview. In reality he is likely to continue to achieve many of these goals, year after year, after first achieving them, for example, having his sketches performed on radio and saving to give up his day job. But these still only go in once on this time plan.

EXERCISE 3: POTENTIAL PITFALLS AND IMPOSSIBLE GOALS

Write down in your contemplation journal:

- any obstacles you expect to encounter that could inhibit you achieving a particular goal – for example, Jack may live somewhere very remote and be unable to attend stand-up classes
- any obstacles you might encounter as you work more generally towards your goals. This could be anything from hurdles such as lack of time to challenges that could have major life consequences, such as your partner being unsupportive of your goals.

For each obstacle, consider and write down in your contemplation journal:

- what influence you have over it
- what you could you do to overcome it
- whether you need to add extra goals to the plan you created in Exercise 1 to overcome this challenge – if so, add them
- whether you need to reconsider or restructure any goals.

If you can't think how to overcome an obstacle, brainstorm nine ideas – Appendix 3 gives guidance on how to perform effective brainstorming. Reflect on the ideas you come up with. If none of them are realistic or practical, consider how you could change or modify them to realistically overcome the obstacle.

Insight

One way to identify how you could overcome an obstacle is to imagine yourself having already overcome it. Use your contemplation journal to consider what has changed about your situation, or about you, once this has happened. Ask yourself what you can do to make that change real.

Insurmountable obstacles

If there is an obstacle that really does make a goal impossible, this is the time to remove it from your agenda and adjust you plans accordingly. However, first reflect on this goal in your contemplation journal, using the following questions:

- Is it really impossible or unrealistic for me to achieve this goal?
- Am I afraid of the consequences of attempting to achieve or actually achieving this goal? If so, are these consequences really as unacceptable as I think they are?
- Do I really want to give up this goal?
- Do I really need to give up this goal?
- Could I leave this goal to one side and consider how to achieve it in the future?
- What values does this goal satisfy?
- How will I satisfy these values in the future?

Add anything else to your reflection that you feel is relevant. Then, if you still think you need to abandon the goal, complete the following sentences in your achievement log:

- I need to leave this goal behind because...
- I am disappointed about this because...
- I am pleased about this because...

Add any further useful reflections that completing these sentences bring to mind. Finally, acknowledge any feelings of sadness you have about letting this goal go.

EXERCISE 4: WRITE DOWN YOUR GOALS

- If you've been sent here from another chapter, write the goal you have come here to work on as a single sentence using the method for formulating goals below.
- If you're not sure which direction you wish to take your writing in, use this exercise to create goals for each area you want to experiment in. Do this by framing each area of experimentation as a sentence in your achievement log using the method for formulating goals below.

- If you know which direction you're taking your writing in, look at the time plan you drew in Exercise 1. Write each of your goals as a single sentence in your achievement log using the method for formulating goals below.

FORMULATING EACH GOAL

- **Make it personal** – This usually means starting your sentence with 'I'. Personal also means the goal should be important to you and exciting – if not, why are you aiming for it?
- **Make it precise** – State exactly what you want and when you will achieve it. For example, don't just say you want to be a novelist, define the genre you will write. Be as specific as you can so you know when you achieve your goal.

COACHING TIPS

Coaching tips

- ✓ Finite facts and figures are ideal for making your goals precise. For example, noting how much you intend to write each day or by when you intend to have written your latest draft.
- ✓ Sometimes there are no finite criteria you can apply. If you have trouble finding a way of making your goal precise, ask yourself, 'How will I know when I've achieved this goal?' If there are no solid measures, consider how you will feel or the changes you will see once you have achieved the goal.
- ✓ Always set a deadline for when you will achieve a goal by. You may not find it easy, but your deadline is only an estimate and can be revised at any time.

- **Make it now** – Write your goal in the present tense, as though you already have it (see examples below).

Insight

If we write a goal in the present tense our subconscious sees it as 'happening' now. It will therefore encourage us to work on that goal and look for solutions to challenges associated with it.

- **Make it positive** – Make sure your goal is written as an entirely positive statement. Statements such as 'I do not have...' and 'I have lost...' can feel like we are asking for something negative to happen to us. If we rephrase a goal positively it will be more attractive and motivational. (See Appendix 2 for more about checking that you are using positive language.)

Examples of goals that are precise, personal, positive and present tense:

- 'I am a romantic novelist publishing one book a year by the time I'm 50.'
- 'I have completed the first draft of my novel by 31 July this year.'
- 'I write 1000 words a day.'

Example of a precise, personal, positive and present tense experimental goal:

- 'I know whether or not I want to be a scriptwriter by 31 December this year.'

Note

Sometimes writing a present tense sentence which talks about something we will achieve in the future sounds clumsy. Do your best to make it smooth, but don't give in to temptation to write it in the future tense.

EXERCISE 5: MAKE SHORT-TERM PLANS

Identify the goals you want to achieve within the next year. Set a deadline for when you would like to (and realistically can) have achieved each of these.

Also identify any actions you need to take in the next year to achieve your longer-term goals. Consider completing these actions as goals for the next year and set a deadline for when you would like to (and realistically can) have achieved them by. Write them down as precise, personal, positive, present tense statements, following the rules in Exercise 4.

Making notes in your contemplation journal, if you find it helpful, work out the main steps you need to take to reach each deadline you have set to achieve this year and when you will need to take each step. Don't get hung up about accuracy as you make your plans, particularly if your goal is dependent on other people such as editors and publishers. For example, if you want to get ten short stories published in a year, you may plan to write four stories a month. However, nothing can guarantee you will get ten published in a year. Under these circumstances you just have to make the best estimate of what you think you need to do to achieve your goal.

EXERCISE 6: MAKE ACTION PLANS

Using your contemplation journal, write down as a goal everything you intend to achieve in the next three months. (Make sure each is written as a precise, personal, positive and present tense statement, following the rules in Exercise 4.) These are your short-term goals.

Work out exactly what actions you need to take during this time to achieve your short-term goals.

Example
Goal: I have submitted six short stories by 31 March this year.

Action plan

- Visit a different public place weekly to take in atmosphere and observe – from w/c 2 January onwards.
- Look through ideas box – 5 January.
- Consult *Writers' & Artists' Yearbook* to find suitable magazines w/c 9 January.
- Study potentially suitable magazines themselves w/c 9 January.
- Send for submission guidelines from suitable magazines w/c 9 January.
- Write one story a week starting w/c 16 January.
- Rewrite as necessary ensuring that if no new story is written in a week, I spend at least five hours a week rewriting.
- Send stories as they are completed.

COACHING TIPS

Coaching tips

- ✓ If you have trouble identifying the actions you need to take, work backwards from the achievement, asking yourself, 'What is the last thing I will have done before I achieve this?' This is also a useful method to use if you have to fit your actions into a certain timeframe.
- ✓ If the actions you need to carry out can't be fitted into the allotted time, move your target date for completion.
- ✓ If the actions must fit the allotted time, or you are not prepared to move the target date, then:
  - ▷ rearrange or remove other activities, or
  - ▷ rearrange the actions you need to take, or
  - ▷ look for a different way of reaching your goal.
- ✓ Don't be so enthusiastic you end up setting unrealistic targets. This will only serve to dishearten you.

✓ When you set goals to grow personal qualities, consider what you will be doing in the future which demonstrates that you have developed that quality sufficiently.

Insight

Personal qualities rarely (if ever) grow at a steady rate or reach a certain level to order. The best you can do is to ensure that you carry out the actions you plan. If you recognize that your efforts aren't having any influence, make a different plan.

Allowing one page for each, transfer each short-term goal you have formulated into your achievement log. Write the action plan for what you need to do in the next three months below it.

Once you have identified what actions you need to carry out, take them at the appropriate time, checking in with your achievement log when you need to. You may find it helpful to note at the start of each week which tasks you need to carry out that week.

IF GOAL SETTING FEELS TOO RIGID

If putting dates on your goals and plans, or even setting a goal, feels constricting, still have a go at it for a few weeks. If you find this chokes your creativity put a date on achieving your goals and forget about them. However, perform a review at the end of three months (see Appendix 1) to check that you have taken sufficient action towards achieving your goals. If you haven't, consider how well you have been using your time and directing your energies, and don't allow yourself to make excuses.

GOALS ARE NOT CAST IN STONE

Remember, goals are flexible. If things don't go as expected, or you see a better plan, it's fine to move the dates you have attached to a goal, or even abandon a goal if it makes sense to. However, don't keep changing your plans just to put off doing something that fazes you. If you find yourself changing your mind and altering course repeatedly, take a look at Chapters 6 and 7 to help address any thinking that is influencing your actions. You may also find Chapter 14 helpful.

I have weekly and monthly writing goals, which I tick off as I complete them. It helps to have these self-imposed deadlines. If I didn't I'd certainly be more complacent.

Della Galton

MOVING ON

Congratulations! You have now set clear goals with in-built motivation to succeed. You have also created an action plan for the next three months. All you have to do now is start following your plans. When you come to the end of the three-month period, turn to Appendix 1, which explains how to carry out a three-monthly review and how to move on from there – don't forget to make a note in your diary to do this! Appendix 1 also explains how to carry out weekly and monthly reviews, if you feel you would benefit from an even more structured approach to staying on top of your goals.

If you are experimenting, once you have clearer ideas of where you want to focus your talents (which may take some time), go back to Chapter 1 and work forward again from there. There will be much that you do not need to repeat, such as identifying values, so work only on the exercises or parts of exercises that are influenced by the decisions experimentation has led you to.

If at any time you get stuck, use the relevant chapters in parts two and three to address the challenges you find yourself facing.

FINAL WORD

Maintaining focus on the future you desire is essential if you want to achieve your goals. Nevertheless, don't be so focused on the future that you forget to enjoy the here and now – also do things that make life rich and fulfilling today.

10 THINGS TO REMEMBER

1 To succeed as a writer you need to find the right balance between focus and maintaining the ability to explore and innovate.

2 Don't get too hung up on timescales when you consider achieving your goals. Nothing is certain when others' approval and opinion is involved.

3 Writing goals includes activities that support your writing ambitions.

4 When considering the obstacles in your way, ensure a goal is truly insurmountable before you let it go.

5 Goals should be precise, personal, positive, present tense and have an action plan attached to them.

6 If you have trouble identifying the actions you need to take to achieve a goal, work backwards from the achievement, asking yourself, 'What is the last thing I will have done before I achieve this?'

7 Personal qualities rarely (if ever) grow linearly, or reach a certain level to order. The important thing here is to ensure you work on them and recognize if your efforts aren't having any influence.

8 If you choose not to set formal goals, decide what you want to achieve over the next three months and review your progress when that three months is up.

9 Goals are flexible. Both your goals and your deadlines will change as you work towards them.

10 Remember to enjoy the here and now and do things that make your life rich and fulfilling today.

What do you think?

In this chapter you will learn:
- *how the way you think can block, demotivate and reduce creativity*
- *how to reduce the detrimental effects of limiting thinking.*

How the voice inside your head could be holding you back

We all have an internal dialogue that chatters away inside our head; discussing things with us, reliving memories, cheering us on and sometimes being downright negative. But how often do you think about the voice itself?

The voice of our thoughts is a great ally when it's encouraging us to write or coming up with a fantastic plotline or character. It's not such a good friend when it's telling us, 'You always write a load of rubbish', 'You'll never make that deadline', 'Nobody will want to read what you write.' However, our internal voice gives us these messages for a very good reason: to keep us safe when it recognizes we're stepping out of our comfort zones.

Our inner dialogue builds its opinion on past evidence and primeval fears. It looks hardest for evidence of the negative that might happen as a result of our actions, past experience of failure, others' anecdotes of disappointment, or perceiving something as hard to accomplish will all trigger doubts. If we've no experience of something, or no information about it, this will also cause feelings of apprehension, because we have no past memories that tell us what to expect or how to react.

Real life

The first novel Gemma had written was rejected by over 20 agents, so she kept telling herself she was wasting her time writing a second novel, because that would be rejected too.

Jacob's first film script was praised so highly, he was sure he'd never be able to make the next one anywhere near as good.

When 'keeping safe' thinking applies to our writing it can reduce creativity and stop us writing. This is because anything that causes anxiety, or warns of possible danger, shifts our brainwaves to the higher end of the attentive beta brainwave state where creativity is low or non-existent. We also lose motivation, because the voice urges caution, not action. Furthermore, internal negativity distracts us from thinking about our writing, by encouraging us to question our abilities and, in doing so, builds even more self-doubt. On top of this, we save these doubts to fuel more internal negative comments next time we focus on our writing. The worst case scenario is that we spiral down into negativity, reducing our motivation and creativity more and more until we stop working on our writing completely.

Coaching experience

Jaz was very excited by an idea he had for a novel. He knew how it started and he knew how it ended. But having written the first three chapters, he realized he knew almost nothing about the middle. He stopped writing and began to consider the midsection.

Having made a few notes about what he thought would happen in the middle, he began to write again. As he wrote, he became distracted by thoughts about how what he was writing would mature in the middle of the story. His thoughts drifted to the few scenes he had identified, but none of them seemed to connect properly.

From then on, every time Jaz sat down to write, his thoughts moved to how empty the midsection of the story felt. He began

(Contd)

to question if he was wasting his time. What if he got to the middle and he didn't know what to write? What if nothing much happened in the middle? What if his novel wasn't long enough?

Jaz wrote two more chapters before the nagging thoughts grew so intrusive he came to a standstill. He looked back over what he had produced already, looking for clues to where he was going. But all this did was lead him to recognize he was deeply unhappy with the last two chapters he had written. He attempted to start Chapter 4 again... and again. But every time he sat down to write, he asked himself what was the point of writing anything if he couldn't get through the midsection. On top of his fears about the middle of the story, he was also now telling himself Chapters 4 and 5 were badly written, and he was questioning whether he had the ability to write a novel at all.

Of course, it's impossible to get rid of our voice of caution. And we wouldn't want to if we could. It does a very good job of keeping us safe; telling us not to put our hand in the fire, not to walk into the middle of the road, to be wary of wild animals with sharp teeth. But when it comes to our writing, there's a lot we can do to reduce and remove the limiting influence of our protective voice and to stop it from holding us back in the future.

What are you thinking?

Even if, like Jaz, we know we are carrying negativity about our writing, it's easy to miss what that negativity is telling us. And, even if we do recognize what it's telling us, it's easy to have further negativity we haven't spotted.

Attempting to fully identify what your inner voice says is tricky, because the moment you consider what you are thinking, you stop thinking your everyday thoughts. However, the following steps are designed to assist you to identify both obvious negativity and potentially unhelpful thoughts that evade you.

STEP 1: CATCHING THE EASY-TO-FIND THOUGHTS

You may be aware of some negativity you hold regarding your writing; thoughts such as:

- 'My writing's not good enough.'
- 'I'll never write a book as good as the last one.'
- 'There are so many other wannabe writers – I don't stand a chance.'

If you recognize that you have any negativity about your writing, write the relevant thoughts down in your contemplation journal.

STEP 2: CATCHING THE NOT-SO-EASY-TO-FIND THOUGHTS

Ask a friend to listen while you explain your current challenges regarding your writing. If you don't have a friend you feel comfortable talking to, you could record yourself talking out loud. Alternatively, you could write your thoughts down in your contemplation journal. Whatever way you choose, aim to get your thinking flowing so that you are less likely to censor what you 'say'.

If you are talking to a friend, ask them to listen rather than offer opinion, even if it is sympathetic. If you are journaling or recording yourself, allow your thoughts to flow without questioning where they come from or censoring them.

Coaching tip

COACHING TIP

- ✓ If you feel self-conscious talking out loud to yourself, record yourself while you're out walking somewhere where there aren't other people, or while you're preoccupied with a routine task, such as housework.

Whatever way you choose to capture your thoughts, when you come to a stop ask, 'What are my current challenges regarding my writing?' (or get your friend to ask each time you stop talking, 'What are your current challenges regarding your writing?') until you truly can't think of any more answers.

Ask your friend to write down – or as you listen to your recording, or review what you have written in your journal, note down – any challenges you identify that impact on your writing, anything you say that sounds negative and particularly note when you use the following words:

- but
- ought, should, could, must
- try, attempt, have a go
- afraid, lack confidence, frightened
- can't, am unable, don't

STEP 3: IF YOU'VE FAILED TO IDENTIFY ANY THOUGHTS THAT UNDERMINE YOUR SUCCESS

If the methods mentioned don't provide you with an insight into any negativity or challenges you recognize, do the following over the next week.

Set a trigger activity of something you do several times a day – preferably an activity you do while you are in the process of working on your writing or thinking about your writing, for example making a cup of coffee. Alternatively you could set an alarm that goes off at certain intervals.

Each time you perform the trigger activity or the alarm goes off, note what you are thinking about. If your thinking is positive, carry on. If you are thinking negatively about your writing, or that you have some sort of writing challenge you need to deal with, make a note in your contemplation journal of exactly what you are thinking and write down any thoughts or concerns you have relating to it.

ANALYZE YOUR THINKING

Review any negative thoughts or challenges you or your friend have identified in Steps 1 to 3. (If you've come here from another chapter, consider the thoughts you have come to 'analyze'.) You may immediately dismiss some of what you have found, because you recognize it is based on ungrounded fears, doubts or obstacles that applied a long time ago, which are no longer applicable to you or your situation. If this is the case for anything you have identified, tell yourself that this is untrue. If you find yourself entertaining these doubts or fears in the future, stop thinking then and remind yourself they are completely untrue.

For any thoughts or challenges you don't immediately dismiss, consider if there is a central message or several main themes. Identify and write these down. Your concerns are likely to relate to something to do with your writing skills and abilities, the consequences of success or failure, or the market you write for.

Coaching experience

Jaz's story continued:

When Jaz considered his thoughts, he identified that his internal negativity told him:

- 'There's no point writing the beginning if you don't know what happens in the midsection.'
- 'Your writing isn't good enough.'
- 'You'll never write a novel.'

Jaz considered the messages he was sending himself. The first thought told him he couldn't write the novel until he knew what happened in the middle. The second two thoughts told him he couldn't write a novel at all. Therefore the message he was giving himself was, 'I can't write a novel.' And that's exactly what he was doing, not writing a novel.

Pick the most persistent or distracting message(s) your inner voice gives you and work on these initially by considering which of the following type of thoughts they are:

Group 1: Thoughts that include 'but'
'But' identifies a reason, or several reasons, why you are not doing something. Whatever reason follows the 'but', take this reason to the section below entitled *What's stopping you?* and use the exercise there to work on it.

EXAMPLES

- I know I should read more, *but* I don't have the time.
- I'd love to write fiction, *but* I'm just not creative enough.

Group 2: Thoughts that include 'ought', 'should', 'could', 'must' or 'have to'
These words suggest either you know you need to do something or you know someone else thinks you should do it, but you aren't doing it. Any time you find yourself saying or thinking any of the these words, ask

yourself, 'What are the reasons I ought/should/could/must/have to do this?' This will lead you to recognize one or two of the following:

- There is something you need or want to do and you just aren't getting round to it. In this case, make a plan to do it and stick to it.
- There is something you believe you need or want to do, however, there's a 'but' telling you it's not possible. In this case use the section *What's stopping you?* below to address the 'but'.
- You are resisting doing something because you think it is someone else's agenda. In this case, consider if there are good reasons to follow that person's agenda.
  - If there are good reasons to follow this person's agenda, place this activity on your own agenda as a 'need' or 'want' to do. Also address any 'but' that is involved by using the *What's stopping you?* section later.
  - If there are no good reasons to follow this person's agenda, each time you hear yourself say you 'should' do this in the future, stop and remind yourself why it is a bad idea. If you keep reminding yourself why you aren't following this course of action, eventually the related thought that you 'should do it' will fade.

Group 3: Thoughts that include 'try', 'attempt' or 'have a go'

These words accept that you may fail at a task before you have even started it. They may just be the way you speak or they may be revealing fear, lack of confidence, other obstacles or a shortcoming you are consciously or subconsciously aware of.

- If these words are simply a matter of the way you phrase things then don't worry about them for now. But if you take a look at Chapter 7, when you've finished this chapter, you will learn how this sort of language – even when not meant negatively – can be detrimental.
- If you recognize that you are using these words because of a shortcoming you have, make a plan to address that shortcoming and take action.
- If you recognize that you are using these words because there are significant obstacles or circumstances that are holding you back, work on the *What's stopping you?* section later.
- If you recognize that these words are linked to fear or lack of confidence, then work on them in the *What's stopping you?* section later.

EXAMPLES

- 'I'll *try* to find more time to write each week.'
- 'I've *had a go* at making my dialogue better, *but* I'm just no good at it.'
- 'I *try* to find peace and quiet to write, *but* with three teenage children and a dog it's impossible.'

Group 4: Thoughts that include 'afraid', 'frightened' or denote lack of confidence

These words show fear or lack of confidence and need to be worked on in the *What's stopping you?* section later.

Group 5: Thoughts that include 'can't', 'am unable' or 'don't'

Saying 'I can't', 'I'm unable', 'I don't' or other similar phrases immediately stops us thinking that we might be able to do or have whatever we are discussing. We therefore stop looking for solutions and stay stuck exactly where we are. Being stuck exactly where we are provides further evidence to our subconscious that we 'can't' do something, which fuels the belief 'we can't' even further.

However, when we say 'I can't', 'I'm unable', 'I don't have' about our writing, we don't usually mean we believe something is completely and utterly impossible or we'll never have it. We usually mean that we don't believe we can do it because of:

- fear or lack of confidence
- our current circumstances
- recognition of significant obstacles, or potential obstacles, standing in our path.

If you've come up with a 'can't', 'am unable', 'don't' or similar, use the *What's stopping you?* section later to deal with it.

EXAMPLES

- 'I *can't* send the manuscript to my agent, she's expecting something funnier.'
- 'I *am* completely *unable* to write deep enough characters.'
- 'I *don't* have enough time to write.'

Insight

If I find myself saying, 'I can't...', I replace it with 'I choose not to...'. This usually makes me recognize that I am in full control of the situation and that I really do have power to change it.

Note

If you've come up with thinking you recognize as negative or challenges that you can't identify as belonging to, or linking to, the groups earlier, take a look at Appendix 2. This gives further examples of words and phrases that can indicate negativity and thinking that is holding you back.

What's stopping you?

Several thoughts you have recorded in the section above may lead you here. You may also have arrived here from another chapter, having identified something that is 'stopping you'. If you've come from another chapter, skip to the next paragraph. If you're making your way through this chapter, for each thought that has led you here ask, 'What's stopping me doing this?' Your answer will either be:

- fear or lack of confidence
- something to do with your circumstances
- an obstacle you perceive as preventing you.

Once you have identified what is stopping you, consider what steps you can take to change this. Ask yourself questions such as, 'How can I beat that fear?', 'How can I become more confident about what I lack confidence over?', 'How can I change my circumstances so they are favourable?', 'How can I overcome this obstacle?' Brainstorm possibilities or discuss with others if it helps – Appendix 3 gives guidance on how to perform effective brainstorming.

Coaching experience

Jaz's story continued:

When Jaz considered the central message he was sending himself, 'I can't write a novel', he realized it was based on a lack of confidence, which was rooted in him not understanding what happened in the middle of his story. Considering how to address this, Jaz recognized that everything he knew about novel writing came from reading books. They had told him writers either plotted or just wrote and saw where it went.

Jaz had already worked on plotting and been unable to find sufficient substance for the middle. He knew he wasn't comfortable just writing and seeing where it went. He therefore decided to learn more about writing by joining a local writing group and talking to other writers about his challenge. He believed this would enable him to gain more than one person's opinion, both about how to write a novel and on his writing itself when he shared his work at their critique meetings. However, Jaz felt intimidated by the idea of attending the group, because he considered everyone who attended would be a 'proper writer' and he wasn't.

HAVE YOU FOUND A SOLUTION?

If you have found a solution and are happy to work on it, go to the next section *Taking action against thoughts that limit success*. If you feel apprehensive or fearful about taking the course of action you believe it would be best to take, read the next section *Fear, apprehension and lack of confidence*. If you're struggling to find a solution consider the following advice.

Sometimes the only obstacle to us not doing something is because we believe it will be hard to achieve, involve a lot of hard work, or it will take a long time accomplish. If this is the case, consider whether the result you're aiming for is something you really want to achieve. If it is, working through Exercises 4 to 6 in Chapter 5 can help you break this goal down into manageable stages.

If you really can't find a way to deal with your writing challenge(s) turn to Exercise 3 in Chapter 5. Take whatever is stopping you as the obstacle(s) you expect to encounter and work through the section *Insurmountable obstacles* within this exercise. If this leads you to decide to abandon addressing the obstacles you have identified, consider the impact abandoning this will have on your writing goals. If something is standing in the way of your writing ambitions, which you truly cannot overcome, you need to reconsider your writing goals and adjust them accordingly.

Insight

Remember, very few things are truly impossible, we just haven't recognized a solution yet or we don't like the solution we see.

FEAR, APPREHENSION AND LACK OF CONFIDENCE

It's normal to feel apprehensive when you are doing something new or stepping out of one of your comfort zones. This is your subconscious's way of keeping you safe.

If you feel fearful or apprehensive about taking a certain course of action, you can explore your concerns further by asking:

- 'What would happen if I didn't do this?' This will help identify whether the consequences of not doing what you're afraid of are worse than doing it.
- 'Why not do it?' Once you have your reason(s) not to do it, ask 'So what?' This will help you recognize whether your fear is keeping you safe from something that has potential repercussions you should be concerned about or whether you are simply afraid of stepping out of your comfort zone.
- 'What comfort zone am I worried about stepping out of?' Once you know this, consider what steps you can take to reduce or remove your underlying fear. Brainstorming may be helpful here – see Appendix 3 for how to perform effective brainstorming.

Even if we don't identify actions we can take to ease or eliminate a fear, simply understanding more about the root of it can make a fear less daunting. Exploration can also occasionally lead us to recognize that it's not a good idea to pursue the solution we have identified.

Real life

Nargis felt too afraid to submit her first novel to an agent. When she asked herself, 'Why not submit it?' her fear answered, 'Because you might get rejected'. She then asked, 'So what?' This led her to recognize getting rejected wasn't such a big deal, she could resubmit elsewhere and that she might get some useful feedback with a rejection.

A FINAL WORD ABOUT FEAR

Getting our writing out there can be a scary experience and there may be times when your fear is right to stop you. However, sometimes we just need to look fear in the eye and take up the gauntlet. After you've done it once, you know you can do it again, only next time you'll have experience to guide you. Once you've broken the fear barrier, it might still not be a breeze, but things will get easier if you keep pushing the boundaries. Your negative voice is fuelled by fear. Get rid of unreasonable fear by facing it.

Insight

Baby steps will take us to our goals as well as giant leaps. I never force myself to do more than I can cope with when I'm pushing boundaries. I just work on each step, one at a time, taking a break if I feel need to.

Taking action against thoughts that limit success

Assuming you haven't decided to abandon taking action to overcome what is stopping you, you'll now have identified a solution to the challenge your inner voice has alerted you to. Check that you are happy with all the potential consequences of taking action, then formulate what you want to achieve by taking this action as a personal, precise, present tense, positive goal:

- **Personal** – This usually means starting your sentence with 'I'.
- **Precise** – State the end result that your solution brings, for example, that you have completed a first draft, or exactly what you will do, for example, write a thousand words a day. Your sentence is therefore likely to start: 'I have…', 'I am…', 'I…' and will have any appropriate finite facts and figures attached to it. Also include when you will achieve your result.
- **Present tense** – Write the sentence as though your solution has already happened.
- **Positive** – Statements such as 'I do not have..' and 'I have lost…' can feel like we are talking about something negative happening to us. They are therefore less attractive and harder to achieve. If we rephrase a goal positively it will be more attractive and motivational. (See Appendix 2 for more about checking that you are using positive language.)

Examples of personal, precise, present tense, positive goals

- 'I have my own website by the end of June this year.'
- 'I write in the library every Tuesday and Thursday evening from 7–9 p.m.'
- 'I have discussed my concerns about my manuscript with my agent by the end this week.'

If you have done the work in Part one, add this statement to your plans as a short-, medium- or long-term goal – depending on how long you expect to take to achieve it – and take the appropriate action. If you haven't done the work in Part one, create a plan to achieve what you want to accomplish and take action at the right times.

Coaching experience

Jaz's story continued:

To implement his solution and overcome his apprehension about joining a writing group, Jaz set the goal, 'I attend a writing group every month.' His action plan included:

- ▶ Remind myself daily that no one is born a writer and we all have to learn.
- ▶ Research possible writing groups to attend.
- ▶ Contact writing group that appears to be the most useful.
- ▶ Attend writing group.

When Jaz joined a writing group, he talked to the group's members about how they wrote and what they knew about writing. They told him exactly what the books he had read said: some people plotted intricately while other didn't even know what the end of their story was. But on top of this, Jaz also heard people tell stories of being fearful of wasting time or of writing an awful novel. Other writers talked about learning by writing and reassured Jaz that there was usually a bit of a muddle in the middle, even for writers who plotted intricately. These insights gave Jaz the confidence to start working again on his novel.

MOVING ON

This chapter has helped you to identify limiting thoughts and how to take action against them. Chapter 7 will show you techniques to reduce and remove the thoughts themselves. It will also assist you to identify and address language that is holding you back and giving negative messages about you to other people.

10 THINGS TO REMEMBER

1. We all have an internal voice that sometimes holds us back and sometimes cheers us on.
2. It's up to you what your internal voice tells you.
3. Limiting thinking plays an important part in keeping us safe.
4. Listen to the language you use to identify where you are blocking and demotivating yourself.
5. It's usually more productive to get a friend to feed back what you say about your writing challenges than to attempt to listen to your own thoughts.
6. Work on your most persistent and distracting limiting beliefs first.
7. You could be held back by thoughts you already know to be untrue.
8. We are usually held back by fear or lack of confidence, circumstances or obstacles we perceive as preventing us.
9. It is natural to feel uneasy when you are stepping out of one of your comfort zones.
10. When you feel afraid to do something, ask yourself, 'Why not do it?' and 'So what?' to help recognize whether your fear is keeping you safe or you are simply afraid of doing something new and unfamiliar.

7

The influence of positive language on positive thinking

In this chapter you will learn:

- ***how what you think and say influences what you achieve***
- ***to use metaphors to address your writing challenges.***

Mind your language

The language we use works in two directions. It doesn't only give away what we're thinking to others, it also travels back in the opposite direction telling us what to think. If you say you're struggling to write, it doesn't just tell the people around you you're struggling to write, it tells *you* you're struggling to write, your subconscious believes you and tries to help you act in that way.

Each time you think or say you're stuck, blocked, lack motivation, are procrastinating, or any other negative, your subconscious will hear you and work to help you make it true. This will perpetuate the negative you are already experiencing and make it harder to work against it. It's therefore not just important to take action against the thoughts that are limiting you, but also to work on the language and the thoughts themselves.

In the future, when you talk about your writing, take note when you hear yourself use any of the language in the groups identified in 'Analyze your thinking', in the *What are you thinking?* section in Chapter 6. Unless you have good reason to maintain the belief, change what you have just said to a positive. For example, change 'can't' to 'can', 'should/ought/must' to 'want' or 'need'.

Good habit

Chapter 6 talked about negativity and negative thoughts. This makes the concept easier to understand. However, referring to negativity in our thoughts as 'negative thinking' or 'negative beliefs', can send a message to our subconscious that our thoughts are bad and that we are a negative person.

Now that you're working to clean up negativity, change your language by calling 'negative thinking' or 'negative beliefs', 'limiting beliefs' or 'limiting thinking'. This describes their function more accurately, which is that they are working to keep you safe and highlighting where you might need to be cautious. This also stops you telling yourself you are a negative person and acknowledges that limiting thoughts are an important part of your brain activity – which you are in control of – and not an invasive beast that's getting the better of you.

Taking positive thinking further

It's important to turn our limiting thinking around and send it back, changing it to a positive when we hear it is not enough. We need to deal determinedly with the thoughts that limit us to stop them returning.

HOW OUR THOUGHTS GROW

Our thoughts are carried within our brains along physical pathways called dendrites. When we focus on a particular idea, the dendrites that carry that idea become stronger. This makes it easier for us to have thoughts related to the idea. The opposite of this is also true. If we don't think about something, the pathways related to that idea waste away and we have to make more effort to bring that idea to our awareness.

The result of the way dendrites are stimulated to grow and diminish, is that the more we ponder our limiting thoughts, the easier it becomes for us to think them and to allow ourselves to become blocked and demotivated. But, if we reduce the amount of time we think a limiting thought, its pathway withers, it becomes physically harder for us to think it and we therefore become naturally less negative, more highly motivated and our writing flows more easily.

To build greater positivity and reduce negativity we therefore need to:

- increase the number of positive thoughts we have
- stop ourselves thinking limiting thoughts.

INCREASING POSITIVE THINKING

By feeding a positive phrase regularly to our brain we can stimulate the growth of the dendrites carrying this positivity.

Step 1: Create a new thought

Consider the most important or most immediate change you want to make and the limiting thought that confronts it. If you've arrived here from another chapter, then consider the limiting thoughts or change you have come here to work on.

- Ask, 'What needs to be true for the opposite of this limiting thought to occur?' For example, the opposite of, 'I am too tired to write in the evening' could be, 'I have plenty of energy to write in the evening.'
- Ensure that your opposite is entirely positive. For example, 'I have plenty of energy to write in the evening' is positive, but 'I am not too tired to write in the evening' suggests we lack something, because it contains the word 'not'. Even though this lack is something we want to lack, it feels less positive than if we create a sentence that states we 'have' something.
- Consider whether there are any other positive opposites you could create to oppose your limiting thought. For the example here you could also have, 'It's a breeze working on my writing in the evening' or, 'I find it easy to work on my writing in the evening.'
- Choose the positive opposite you like best, or feel most comfortable with, to oppose your limiting thought.

COACHING TIP

Coaching tip

✓ If you have already worked on the change you are addressing in Chapter 6, the personal, present tense, positive, precise sentence you created there can be used as your positive opposite.

Step 2: Find evidence

Now look for evidence that backs up your positive opposite. For the example above you might ask, 'When have I had enough energy to write in the evening?' or 'When have I been able to concentrate on an intellectual task in the evening?' Uncovering this should allow you to believe you can make your positive opposite true.

Coaching experience

If you read Jaz's story in Chapter 6, you may remember that he held three main negative beliefs:

- 'There's no point writing the beginning if you don't know what happens in the midsection.'
- 'Your writing isn't good enough.'
- 'You'll never write a novel.'

The encouragement Jaz's writing group gave him dispelled his belief that there was no point writing anything if he didn't know what happened in the midsection. However, he still held the beliefs, 'Your writing isn't good enough' and, 'You'll never write a novel'.

Jaz counteracted these with the simple positive, 'My writing is good enough for me to write a novel.' He backed this idea up with the evidence that his writing group had seen the first chapter of his novel and told him that he wrote well.

Step 3: Confront your thinking

Repeat your positive opposite 50 times a day to embed the new belief in your subconscious and help chase out the old one. As you repeat your new belief, remind yourself of any evidence to support it and of any action you are taking to make it true. Keep repeating the new belief 50 times daily until it becomes true.

Coaching tip

COACHING TIP

✓ A good time to perform your repetitions is when you are doing a repetitive activity that you don't need to concentrate on too hard,

(Contd)

such as jogging. Even if you don't link your repetitions to an activity, deciding on a time of day when you will do them is a good idea to make sure you don't forget.

Step 4: If your brain answers back

If your positive opposite is met by your brain throwing new concerns straight back that contradict it, create more positive opposite(s) to address these concerns. This is one reason it's best to work only on the most important or most immediate change you want to make at present. Otherwise you could end up with a long list of positive opposites that stop you being as direct as possible with your internal voice.

Once you are happy that you are feeling sufficiently positive about a challenge, work on the next most important or most immediate change you want or need to make.

Insight

Initially you may find that, when you repeat your positive opposite(s), you give yourself a reply that says you don't believe yourself. If this is the case, say 'I can…', 'I am learning to…', 'I am improving…' or something similar, rather than 'I am…', to make your statement(s) more believable.

Coaching experience

It isn't just our beliefs about our writing that influence our writing. Aspiring scriptwriter Raj was struggling to decide which character's point of view he wanted to tell his story from. When he listened to the voices that were stopping him, he realized that he held a general belief that he couldn't make decisions.

Having spent time considering this belief, Raj concluded that he easily made decisions he considered unimportant, but got bogged down with decisions he thought were important. He also recognized that he could never be completely sure he was making the right decision over anything, because that's the way life is.

Raj's reflection freed him up to decide to work on a particular point of view in his writing, rather than wasting time wrestling with indecision. He also decided that in future, if he couldn't decide what to do regarding his writing, he would simply plump for one choice and explore it. Furthermore, he reminded himself that whatever decisions he made regarding his writing, they weren't life-or-death decisions and he could always change his mind.

A bonus of the work Raj did on his writing beliefs was to recognize how indecisive he was in the rest of his life. This allowed him to work on strategies to help him reduce this too.

In the future when Raj heard a voice telling him he couldn't make important decisions, he challenged it with the positive opposite, 'I can make important decisions', and he reminded himself of all the important decisions he had made in the past.

BLOCKING LIMITING THINKING

You can also take advantage of the way dendrites weaken when they are not stimulated by making a conscious effort to stop thinking limiting thoughts.

Each time you hear a familiar limiting thought, refuse to allow it your attention. If you are alone you can also reinforce this refusal by doing one of the following:

- clapping loudly
- pinching yourself
- saying 'NO' very firmly
- counting to ten
- putting an elastic band on your wrist and 'pinging' it when you hear the thought
- creating a visualization – for example, sticking your fingers in your ears and telling the thought you're not listening.

After you've refused to entertain the thought, shift your thinking onto something positive and preferably unrelated. Repeat this every time you hear a thought that is working against you. It might take a while but, given time, this method will erode the limiting thoughts, because you're physically breaking down the pathways that carry the negativity.

COACHING TIP

Coaching tip

✓ If you've previously created a positive opposite for the limiting thought you're confronting, repeat that to yourself each time you stop the thought – out loud if possible. This will help strengthen your positivity at the same time as you reduce negativity.

RECOGNIZING MORE LIMITING LANGUAGE

Appendix 2 provides a summary of the limiting language already considered in Chapters 6 and 7. It also identifies further limiting language to look out for and eliminate once you've become familiar with the techniques for dealing with it as explained in Chapters 6 and 7. It also gives a quick reference guide to challenging what you hear and offers suggestions of replacement positives.

Symbolic language: using metaphors to increase success and address your challenges

The use of metaphors allows us to express and give form to complex feelings, behaviours, situations and ideas, which we would otherwise find difficult or impossible to explain. Expressing how we feel about our writing in the form of a metaphor can help us understand our feelings more easily, connect more fully to our writing process and address any challenges we are having within that process.

Metaphors are expressed in symbolic language, which is able to 'slip past' the conscious mind and connect to our emotional subconscious rather than our rational conscious. Because metaphors work in this way, they can be used to increase subconscious motivation and address challenges we are experiencing.

DEVELOPING A SUITABLE METAPHOR

Ask yourself, 'How do I feel about the writing project I am currently working on?' Write down all the words that come to mind, for example, energized, fed up, curious, blocked, flowing. You may find that some of your explanations are metaphors already, for example, 'I'm dragging myself up a never-ending mountain'. This is fine. Just write down how you feel in the words that come to you.

When you have completed your list, sit down and relax. Consider each word or phrase on your list, one at a time, and the feelings that generated it. Decide exactly what you meant by each word or phrase. For example, if you feel energized by what you are writing, consider exactly what it feels like. Perhaps you would describe it as the buzz you feel at the end of a session in the gym, the intoxication of being inspired by a piece of music, or the exhilaration of waking on a sunny morning. Or perhaps if you are struggling with a project, maybe it feels like you're pushing against a brick wall, swimming against the tide, wading through treacle, stuck in a swamp, or suffocating.

Note

If you started off with one or more metaphors on your list, you may have modified it, changed it completely or still have it exactly the way you thought of it in the first place. All of these are fine.

Insight

When you consider your feelings, don't worry about what other people would think, just focus on what you think or know it feels like. For example, you might consider your excitement for a project as being like climbing a sheer rock face, while someone else may describe their struggle to write as climbing a sheer rock face. It all depends on how you feel about rock climbing.

Once you have several metaphors about your writing, choose the one that fits best how you feel at the moment, or combine more than one to create a single metaphor. Visualize this as a short 'film' in your mind's eye, reshaping it until it really feels right.

Coaching experience

Here are some metaphors created by my clients:

Limiting thoughts

Phil imagined his unsupportive thoughts as black rain clouds. He watched the rain stop, the clouds become lighter then float away, leaving a clear blue sky.

Loss of motivation

When Eva got bored with redrafting a project, she visualized herself as a bird sitting on its nest hatching its eggs. This reminded her that she needed to sit on one clutch of eggs at a time and for a sufficient time if they were to hatch.

(Contd)

Building creativity
Manik worked on increasing his creativity by imagining his ideas as giant fireworks exploding across the night sky.

Building on positivity
Willem saw his writing as exploring a chest he had found in an old attic. He imagined himself looking through it with each object he found being more intriguing than the last.

When your words don't flow
Having found herself stuck in the middle of her novel, Susan used a visualization of her characters taking a rest at a crossroads then getting up and heading confidently off in the right direction. This helped her writing flow and reduced panic about getting stuck.

Rejection
Every time Sian received a rejection letter she imagined the letter folding itself into a step along with all the past rejection letters she had received. She watched herself walk up the steps to a door. The door opened and she stepped inside a room where a bright light shone on bookshelves full of books she had written.

Time
To stop herself wasting time and taking things too slowly, Maria created a visualization of time slipping from a hole in her pocket. She then saw herself sewing up the hole by getting on with things more quickly.

Procrastination
To encourage himself to stop procrastinating, Adrian visualized himself firing an arrow and it flying straight to the bull's-eye on a straw target.

VISUALIZING YOUR METAPHOR

Visualize the metaphor you have created daily, engaging all your senses and really feeling it as you do so. The more personal and vivid a metaphor is, the greater impact it is likely to have on your thinking.

FINAL WORD

If you've worked your way here from Chapter 1, you have now placed your foundations for writing success. Shoring them up and maintaining them will be an ongoing process, but you have now completed the initial stages of looking at and working on what you want, who you are and what you think. Congratulations!

10 THINGS TO REMEMBER

1. Your subconscious believes what you tell it and works to help you make it true.
2. Use positive language as often as you can.
3. By increasing positive thinking, you make it physically harder for your brain to have limiting thoughts.
4. You can create new positive thoughts to help remove limiting ones.
5. Always look for evidence to back up positive thoughts you create.
6. If you struggle to believe a positive opposite you create, develop more positive opposite(s) to address the concerns your disbelief raises.
7. Limiting beliefs from other areas of your life can hold back your writing.
8. By stopping yourself thinking limiting thoughts, you make it physically harder for your brain to have those limiting thoughts.
9. Metaphors can be used to help address your challenges and to increase positivity and motivation.
10. The more personal and vivid a metaphor is, the greater impact it is likely to have on your thinking.

Part two
Motivation and creativity

8

Boosting motivation

In this chapter you will learn:

- ***different ways to increase motivation for your writing goals.***

When we build motivation into our plans and activities, it works silently to maintain interest and enthusiasm with little need for conscious effort; creativity flows more easily, procrastination and being blocked are the furthest thing from our thinking, we find time to write more easily and rejection is less likely to deter us. Maintaining good motivation isn't just about getting on with our writing, it's key to preventing writing challenges arising.

As we are all individuals, what motivates each of us will be different. Therefore, when you check out the exercises below, some will be more appealing to you and some will work better than others. Take a look and see what inspires you. Some exercises are aimed at helping you identify what motivates you on a personal level, others are simply suggestions of activities you can carry out that you may or may not find helpful.

Motivation and positive thinking

If you wish to build strong long-term motivation, the best first step is to address your thinking, because our thinking underpins everything we do or don't do. Chapters 6 and 7 show you how to explore your thoughts and make them more positive and therefore more conducive to getting on with your writing and writing-related tasks. If you wish to leave Chapters 6 and 7 and work only on this chapter, or work on this chapter first, you will still find techniques to boost your motivation and build good long-term incentives. But remember, if you don't address your thinking, it will continue to influence your motivation.

If you have already done the work in Chapter 6, use the three-step process at the start of the section *What are you thinking?* to identify any thoughts you have missed that relate to your motivation. If you find you have remaining negativity that is influencing your enthusiasm to write, work on it as you did the limiting thoughts you previously identified.

Twenty ways to boost your motivation

1 *ROUTINES AND HABITS*

When we build routines into our lives, we take the actions in those routines unquestioningly. Creating a writing habit or routine will not only help you to write regularly, but also to slip into the mindset to write more easily.

The best way to create a routine is to consider:

- where you can fit a routine into your current daily/weekly structure
- what time(s) of day you are most productive/most creative.

The ideal routine is to write every day at your most productive/creative time, and you're likely to be doing that already, if you can. If you're not, have a good think about how you could rearrange your daily structure. Often we carry on with our life routines not thinking that we can change them. Can you create more space at your optimum writing time? If you can't, don't worry – we often think we have a 'best writing time', but if we build a routine of writing at another time, we can be just as productive at the new time.

Insight

When my children were small I wrote in the evenings, while they were in bed, and believed this was my optimum writing time. Once they were older and went to bed later, I got up early to write. Since then I have considered early morning my most creative time.

Coaching tips

- ✓ You may find it helpful not just to develop a writing routine, but also to develop a separate creativity routine. This way you have a time each day when you write and a different time each day that you devote to purely thinking about your writing.
- ✓ Having a routine doesn't mean doing the same thing at the same time every day.

COACHING TIPS

Before I was published I only wrote at weekends.

Marcus Sedgwick

Once you've considered your routines and your most productive writing and creative times, decide how you can regularly fit writing into your life. If you come up with a routine that is different each day or each week, you may find it useful to write down a plan of how that routine works until it is established. Whatever routine you decide on, ensure that you follow it as closely as possible until it becomes second nature.

Event-orientated routines

If you recognize that it's impossible to create a time-orientated routine, identify what circumstances have to occur for you to be able to find space to write. Ensure that you have the tools you need to write with you at these times, so that you can always take advantage of them.

Real life

When novelist Emma's daughter was at nursery for just two hours twice a week, she developed the writing routine of dashing home the moment she dropped her daughter into the nursery. She wrote furiously for almost two hours, until it was time to leave to pick her daughter up again.

Dan always ensured he kept pens and a notebook in his car, so he would be able to write while he waited for the kids, when he was picking them up from their various after-school activities.

Still struggling to create a routine?

If you find it completely impossible to build up any sort of routine, some of the ideas in Chapter 11 may help you build some form of rhythm into your writing and creativity.

2 *TRIGGERS*

Triggers remind us of previous occurrences. For example, we all have the experience of smelling something that reminds us of a past event. In this case the smell is acting as a trigger.

Triggers can influence us on both a conscious and subconscious level, so they are a great tool for reminding us to write and pulling us effortlessly into our writing or creativity zone. Suitable triggers could be:

- something you do just before you write, such as make a cup of tea, tidy your desk, feed the dog
- objects placed in your writing environment, such as pictures, books and ornaments will remind you visually that this is your writing environment. They don't have to be writing-orientated objects, just whatever tells you this is your space for writing/creating
- listening to a particular type of music
- burning aromatherapy oil as you write
- something you wear while you're writing.

Triggers are also likely to set themselves if you regularly write in the same environment. For example, if you establish a routine of working in a coffee shop each morning, everything around you, the voices, the smell of the coffee, the heat of the cup in your hand, the chair and the table you sit at, the decor and the staff themselves will all become subconscious triggers. Assuming you are productive in the first place, the coffee shop environment will naturally pull you into the zone and encourage you to write once you've been working there a while.

COACHING TIPS

Coaching tips

✓ Don't stop at having one trigger – the more the better. But don't allow your triggers to be so distracting that they take you away from your creative space.

✓ If you set more than one trigger, choose triggers that influence different senses so they have a broader impact.

- ✓ You can make triggers that are project-specific to remind yourself of particular characters, plot or subject matter, for example, listening to particular music, especially something that your character(s) might listen to.
- ✓ Combining a routine with setting triggers will have an even stronger impact on your subconscious motivation.
- ✓ If you are unable to write regularly in the same space, you can still set triggers that are related to your writing and pull you into the zone, such as using a particular type of notebook or savouring the act of opening your laptop case.

Random triggers

Another type of trigger is to use something you do randomly, or that occurs irregularly in your environment. For example, you could use birds as a trigger by deliberately thinking about your writing when you see one. After a while you'll think about your writing whenever you see a bird without having to remind yourself to.

3 *CREATE A FAVOURABLE ENVIRONMENT*

Ensure that your environment is comfortable to work in, especially that there is sufficient light, your posture is good while you are sitting and that there is minimal chance of distraction. You can make your environment even more motivational by surrounding yourself with stimuli that make you feel positive and connected to your writing. This is effectively the same as setting triggers, because after a while these stimuli will act as triggers.

4 *STEP INTO THE FUTURE*

Get excited about what you are creating by engaging with the medium you want to be published in before you achieve it.

Imagine the future

Identify your ultimate writing ambition. Consider what specific events will show you you've achieved this and how achieving it will influence your day-to-day life. Sit quietly and picture what you've identified, running the images in your mind's eye. Connect to this visualization as fully as you can, engaging all your senses and really feeling the excitement and enjoyment of what's happening. Once you've created this short 'film' of your future and future events, keep connecting, exploring and growing it to maintain your enthusiasm.

Real life

When Darla visualized her first book launch in the future, as well as picturing her friends and family celebrating with her in her local bookshop, she imagined the feel of her dress, her excitement, hearing the click of her high-heeled shoes, the taste and feel of champagne fizzing on her tongue and the smell of her new book.

See the future

Create a collage of pictures from magazines that relate to achieving your goals. If you can draw, you may also want to create your own images of yourself accomplishing things you haven't achieved yet.

Write the future

1. Write a letter to yourself in the present tense about what you want to achieve. Read it through really believing you have achieved it. Alternatively, you could write your achievement as a story or biography. You could also read your letter/story/biography out loud or make a recording of it.
2. Create a short sentence that describes a future achievement. For example, 'I am a bestselling author of romantic fiction.' Write this on a small piece of card and use it as a bookmark, so you see it regularly. Write it in the present, not the future, tense as this stimulates your subconscious more powerfully.

Touch the future

Collect objects that relate to the medium you want to be published or performed in, for example books, DVDs, magazines, cinema tickets, programmes, TV schedules. Close your eyes and explore these objects with your fingertips while imagining you have written what they contain or refer to.

Insight

I love to go into bookshops and libraries and work out where the books I want to publish belong on the shelves. I imagine my book sitting between the other books then pick up a book and imagine that it's the book I'm working on.

5 STOP PUTTING UP WITH THINGS

From squeaky doors to unreasonable work colleagues, tolerating people and situations sucks away our enthusiasm and creative flow.

Take out your contemplation journal and list anything and anyone who isn't having a positive impact on your life and your writing. Once you've made your list, plan when and how you are going to address each of these situations.

Taking action may just mean getting on with chores you've been putting off. However, it could mean making life uncomfortable in the short-term, taking major life steps, or spending time and money you can ill afford. Before you take steps to address these sorts of challenges, you need to decide if you really want to address them, because you will need to be prepared to accept any possible consequences that arise from you taking action. If you decide not to do anything about these, when they stress you in the future, remind yourself of the reasons you're allowing the situation to persist. This should help reduce their negative impact.

6 *NEGATIVE PEOPLE*

Are there people in your life who constantly see things negatively, dragging you down into negativity with them? Remove this drain on your motivation in the following manner. Next time they start complaining, listen to them until they repeat themselves. When they reach this point, sympathetically ask how they could find a solution, or get them to consider if there is anything positive about what they are telling you. If you continue to behave like this each time they moan, they'll learn to become less negative or find someone else to complain to.

If there is a reason you have to stay in an environment with negative people and are unable to nudge them to become more positive, create some psychological distance by doing one or more of the following:

- Visualize that you are inside an invisible bubble that protects you from their negativity. Imagine their words and even their energy bouncing away as it hits the bubble, then focus on what you're doing and ignore them.
- Imagine protective music playing all around you, dissolving their negativity.
- Imagine yourself as a positivity superhero pushing their energy away from you. You could make this device more personal by devising your own metaphor for deflecting negativity. See the section *Symbolic language: using metaphors to increase success and address your challenges* in Chapter 7.

Note

None of us are constantly cheerful. If you're not in a good place, have a grumble then look for the positive in the situation and/or work out how to deal with what's bothering you. You may also find it useful to create a metaphor for dispelling your own negativity and becoming more positive.

7 *OTHER NEGATIVE INFLUENCES*

All input influences us. Consider how you can you cut down any negativity generated by, for example, the media while ensuring you don't lose touch with reality.

8 *ADD POSITIVITY*

Spend time with positive people, especially ones who are going to be supportive and positive about your writing and achieving your writing ambitions.

9 *IF YOU FEEL GUILTY ABOUT WRITING*

Just like the other negative influences that impact on us, guilt saps creativity and erodes motivation by reducing our positivity. For writers, guilt is also often a double-edged sword; we feel guilty for neglecting our writing when we're not writing and guilty for leaving other tasks when we are writing.

Consider your guilt

Score on a scale of 1 to 10 how important your writing is to you. (10 = It's top priority, 1 = I'm happy to fit it in after everything else.) Write down the score in your contemplation journal then, for the next week:

- When you're writing and you hear yourself thinking, 'I should be ... instead of writing', note down what it is you think you should be doing.
- When you're not writing and hear yourself thinking, 'I should be writing', make a note of whatever task it is you are doing.

At the end of the week consider what activities you've noted down. Score on a scale of 1 to 10 how important each activity is to you. (Once more 10 = It's top priority, 1 = I fit it in after everything else.) Compare how the priority you've given your writing compares with each of the priorities you've assigned to these other tasks. In future, plan your activities according to how important they are, making sure your writing takes its true place among your list of priorities.

Just knowing you're tackling your priorities appropriately can be sufficient to stop feelings of guilt. But, if you continue to feel guilty about spending time on pursuits that are more important to you than writing, or about leaving tasks of lower importance, simply remind yourself of your priorities, and the reasons for those priorities, each time you feel guilty. When you've done that, refocus on the task in hand. If you start feeling guilty again, continue to remind yourself of your priorities and refuse to listen to the guilty thoughts.

Coaching tips

- ✓ Check occasionally to ensure that your priorities haven't changed and your feelings of guilt aren't reflecting this.
- ✓ If you have trouble ignoring guilty thoughts, the section *Taking positive thinking further*, in Chapter 7, explains how to increase positive thinking and block unwanted thoughts.

10 *RELAX, REST AND REGENERATE*

Taking sufficient time to relax, rest and regenerate is an important part of ensuring our motivation remains high. To identify the right sort of breaks to take, make a list of all the activities you do to:

- relax and unwind
- have fun
- take part in new experiences.

Consider everything from a couple of minutes daydreaming to taking a holiday or bungee jumping for charity.

Over the next month, use your contemplation journal to keep track of how often you take part in these activities and score, on a scale of 1 to 10, how fully you feel they recharge your batteries. (10 = I feel 100% recharged and raring to go, 1 = It made no difference.) Also consider experiences you take part in less regularly, such as holidays, and score how fully they revitalized you.

For anything you have awarded a score of less than five, consider the reasons this score is so low. How could you increase the benefit you gain? Do you want/need to be doing this activity? Could you be taking part in a more nourishing experience instead?

For anything that scores five, six or seven ask, 'What can I do to make this activity more reenergizing?' This could simply mean engaging more fully in what you are doing or it could involve making changes or taking more practical steps. For example, if you love shopping, but go shopping with someone who is often grumpy, you could find a more positive shopping partner, shop alone, or help your friend address their challenges.

Getting the most out of your breaks

- Engage as fully as possible, ensuring you are present in the moment with the experience you are taking part in. Don't drift off into worrying that you are not being productive or worry that you should be attending to other parts of your life.
- Regularly consider what new activities you could add to your list or how you could change some of them to make them feel fresh again. However, don't abandon anything that really nourishes you just for the sake of doing something different.

When to work and when to play

The most useful number of breaks you need to take will vary with what else is happening in your life and with your writing. Regularly pay attention to your life balance, considering all the current influences on you, activities you are involved in, the state of your health and general state of being. Consider the impact these are having on your motivation. Learn to recognize when you need to write, when you need to rest and when you need to spend time getting on with other 'life' activities (even the non-'nourishing' stuff). Don't beat yourself up about not writing when you're not writing. But equally don't keep constantly telling yourself it's 'okay not to write today'. Be honest with yourself and find a balance that truly works for you by listening to your own mind and body, the life you lead.

11 *REMIND YOURSELF OF YOUR ACHIEVEMENTS*

Creating a collection of 'positives' relating to your writing provides you with a physical reminder of your achievements.

Collect:

- copies of your own published work
- unpublished writing you're really pleased with or that tells you something about how your writing has grown

- rejection letters that give positive feedback or acknowledgement
- anything that relates to your writing success or progress. If you can't physically put it in your collection, take a photograph.

If you haven't yet reached a stage in your writing that provides you with anything to put in your collection, list all the things you like or think are good about your writing. You could also add a list of things that are good about being a writer.

Once you've got your collection together, decide what to keep it in. This can be a box or folder, or anything that seems right for you. Find something that you really like the look or feel of, and give it a name you find appealing. This will make it more personal, more attractive and you'll be less likely to forget to look at it.

Insight

One of my clients put her collection in a funky purple shoebox and called it her Passionate Purple Shoe Box. Another client used a First Aid tin, because it made her feel better when she was feeling negative.

Review your box every other month and when you feel despondent or lack motivation. Use it to:

- reflect on how far you've come on your writing journey
- re-imagine the excitement of your achievements, engaging as fully as possible with all your senses and feelings
- remind yourself how much you enjoy writing.

12 *NOTE YOUR ACHIEVEMENTS*

Not only can it take a long time to create a single piece of work, such as a book or film script, it can also take a long time for writers to achieve any obvious success. On top of that, once writers are successful, they are constantly having to prove themselves over and over again with each new project they produce. This makes it easy to lose sight of what you've achieved both on a short- and long-term basis. Logging your achievements can help reduce this sense that you're failing to achieve by enabling you to recognize that you really are making progress.

Short-term achievement

At the end of each day, note in your contemplation journal what you have done that relates to your writing goals. If you have trouble remembering, check what you have done halfway through the day, or even note down what you do each time you do something different.

At the end of each day, review how much you have done. This will help you to recognize your efforts and that you are making daily progress. Look again at your week's activities at the end of each week. This should remind you that you really have done something to progress your writing dreams and worked hard at becoming a successful writer. If it doesn't, review if you really are doing enough.

Coaching experience

Comedy writer Jane decided to note her achievements each day and review them at the end of each week. She found this had a powerful effect on her motivation, because she recognized she had always done much more than she gave herself credit for.

COACHING TIPS

Coaching tips

If you feel you've been struggling with the same chapter, scene or piece of writing for a long time, check back through your notes. You will find that either:

- ✓ It only feels that way and you haven't really been working on it that long – knowing this should help revitalize your motivation.
- ✓ You really have been working on it a long time. If this is what you discover, take a mental step back and consider how you have been spending your time. Has what you've been doing been productive or are you going round in circles? Do you need to take a break and work on something else, then come back with a fresh eye? Do you need to take some other course of action within the writing itself? Do you need to learn something more – either about the craft of writing or about what you are writing?

Long-term achievement

Draw a horizontal line on a piece of paper. At one end write the first step you took to taking your writing seriously. At the other end write a short definition of your ultimate writing goal.

Take out your contemplation journal and write down the steps you have taken so far to achieve your ultimate goal, any obstacles you have overcome and your writing successes. Decide which of these are most significant and mark them on your line in chronological order relative to the start and finish points you have created.

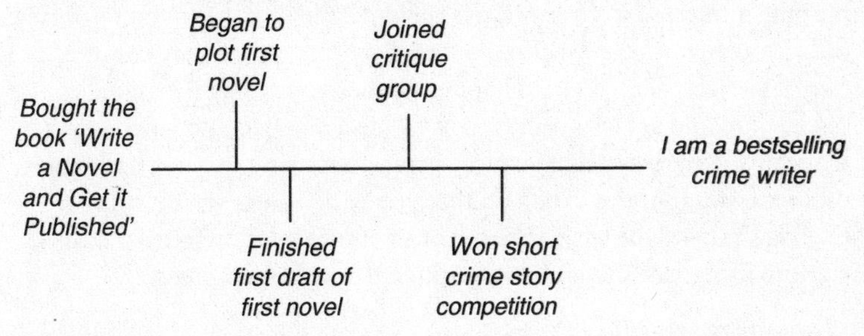

Figure 8.1 Timeline.

It's impossible to truly know how close you are to achieving your ultimate goal, so mark events up to at least a third of the way along the line – even if you feel you are close to the beginning of your journey. This timeline is an acknowledgement of your progress, not an exact measure of how close you are to your ultimate goal.

As you achieve further success and take more actions towards achieving your writing goals, note the most significant on your timeline. If it becomes cluttered or you run out of room to add actions/achievements, remake it, taking out the events that now seem less significant.

Build motivation by using your timeline to remind yourself that you are taking action and making progress towards achieving your writing dreams.

Coaching tips

COACHING TIPS

- ✓ You can make your timeline more visually stimulating, and therefore more inspirational, by writing your achievements and your ultimate goal in different colours or drawing pictures of them.
- ✓ If you enjoy setting goals, you can create timelines for individual goals and/or to track your progress throughout each year.

Insight

It can take a long time to achieve your writing goals. Ensure that when you reflect on your achievements, you celebrate the action you have taken and any positive results those actions have achieved. Don't reflect on what you haven't achieved.

13 *GET OTHERS INVOLVED*

Tell friends and family about your plans. The minute you spread the word that you are working on a project, people who care about you become interested in your progress. They'll then ask how you're getting on. If you've not been working on your writing, when they enquire, one of two things is likely to happen. Either you will feel inspired to dig back in and get to work, or you will feel bad because you haven't made any progress. Being inspired gets you moving. Feeling bad won't motivate you, but it will flag up that you're allowing your writing to slide. If this is the case, take out your contemplation journal and explore the reasons you're not working towards your goals.

More specifically, if you've done the work in Chapters 1 to 5 on setting goals and deadlines, you can tell someone about these and ask them to check up on you. Tell them they need to be hard and not allow you to make excuses, but ensure they understand not to be harsh when you fail to achieve a goal because of factors that are not within your control. If you wish, you can also ask them to help you identify how to overcome obstacles when they arise.

COACHING TIPS

Coaching tips

- ✓ Remember that achieving writing goals can take a long time. If you find it embarrassing telling friends or family you've been rejected (again) then this will not be a good form of motivation for you.
- ✓ Even if this form of motivation works well, be careful not to tell people who won't understand just how long it can take to achieve your writing goals. Their lack of understanding won't have a positive impact.
- ✓ Writers' groups can be a great way of getting others involved as you should all understand the realities of the writing business. Writers' groups can also offer advice and feedback on your work. The section *Taking it further* at the end of this book has more information about writing groups.

As a member of the Society of Children's Book Writers and Illustrators I've been cheered on by other members when things have gone well. They've also listened to my gripes and given me advice. I think as well, seeing other members succeeding demonstrates that getting published isn't a pipe dream.

Jon Mayhew

14 *CELEBRATE YOUR SUCCESSES*

Take time to celebrate each of your writing successes. Reflect on what you have accomplished and savour the feeling of completion. This will refresh and renew your enthusiasm to continue with your next goal. For bigger achievements have a proper celebration or reward.

Coaching tips

- ✓ Celebrate minor milestones within bigger projects as well as completion of the project itself.
- ✓ Reflecting yearly or six monthly on your progress can be an excellent way to ensure you celebrate success regularly – Appendix 1 discusses how to review your progress at regular intervals.

15 *SMALL STEPS*

Most people find their New Year's resolutions are too hard to fulfil, because they are too big and too vague. Even if you haven't set goals, always break what you want to achieve into small, concrete objectives and have a plan of how you're going to achieve them.

16 *QUOTES*

Find quotes that really resonate with you and inspire you. Write them down or print them out and put them where you can see them. Change the quote at least once a month, to keep it fresh, or it will start to blend into the background.

17 *GET RID OF MENTAL CLUTTER*

Constantly having unfinished writing projects in the periphery of our awareness creates mental clutter. This demotivates us by unnecessarily taking up attention and mental energy. It can also drain our creativity. Dealing with these projects or putting them further out of our awareness can help reduce the impact they have on our motivation.

Dealing with mental clutter

Take out your contemplation journal and list which projects are nagging at you but you're not getting on with. Beside each one note the following:

- ▶ What you need to do to complete it and how long you think that will realistically take.

- What has stopped you completing the project previously.
- How completing the project will support your writing goals and ambitions. Also note if it is the only project that can support your writing goals and ambitions in this way.
- Your enthusiasm for the project on a scale of 1 to 10. (10 = I'm really excited, 1 = I've no interest at all.)
- If you have identified your core values (Chapter 3), which values the project fulfils.

Use what you have learned from this investigation to help you prioritize your unfinished projects, both compared with each other and in comparison with anything you are currently working on. Your reflection should lead you to recognize which you wish to continue and which you need to abandon.

Once you have identified which project has top priority, create an action plan of how and when you are going to perform the activities required to complete it. If there are any obstacles that have stopped you working on it in the past, decide how you will overcome them if there is a possibility they will arise again – add this to your plan. Also set a completion date, remembering that it's fine to change this date later on if you have good reason.

Work on your chosen project and leave anything you have decided not to work on. If your thoughts drift to concerns that you should be working on something else, remind yourself that you're currently tackling your top priority and you will work on the next priority when you have time.

When you find time to bring in another writing project, reassess the priorities of your outstanding projects again, along with any new projects you want to work on, then make a plan to complete your top priority/priorities.

Note

Mental clutter can also be caused by outstanding activities from the rest of your life nagging for attention. If this is the case, consider the priority the outstanding jobs have in relation to your writing and whether you should be dealing with them instead. If you struggle to prioritize your writing within the context of the rest of your life, or you feel guilty about writing, see suggestion 9 above.

18 *CREATE A METAPHOR AND VISUALIZE IT REGULARLY*

Chapter 7 discusses creating metaphors to increase motivation as well as for addressing other concerns. See the section *Symbolic language: using metaphors to increase success and address your challenges*.

Insight

When I created a metaphor of wearing magic shoes to boost my flagging motivation, I actually put on my favourite pair of pink shoes. I closed my eyes and imagined hearing the heels click together, magic sparkling from them and a sense of excitement growing inside me.

19 *SET WRITING GOALS*

If you've completed the exercises in Chapters 1 to 5, you will have already begun to build motivation into your writing by creating writing goals and making plans to achieve them. If you haven't done so, you can head there at any time to help increase your long-term motivation.

20 *LINK YOUR GOALS TO YOUR VALUES*

If you have worked through Chapters 1 to 5 you will also already have taken steps to ensure that you have strong motivation to complete your goals by linking them to your values. If you haven't, Chapter 3 will show you how to indentify your core values.

Once you have created a personal core values list, you can compare how your values link to what you are writing. Reflect on the importance of what you are doing and consider how to use them to boost your motivation further.

Coaching experience

Maria had a brilliant idea for a book. She had written a proposal and gained a publisher's interest. However, the publisher wanted her to make serious changes to the proposal and she was unsure whether the result would be a book she really wanted to write.

(Contd)

Finding herself unable even to produce a new proposal, Maria turned to me for coaching, saying she felt no enthusiasm to write the book, even though she recognized that it had great potential. She also said that writing the book would be a 'tedious and time-consuming nightmare'.

Having elicited Maria's core values, I encouraged her to consider how the book itself and the process of writing it connected with her values. In doing this Maria realized that ten of her 12 core values were linked to the project. This helped her recognize how important the book was to her and how exciting it really was. Knowing her values also helped Maria to work out how to bring more of them into the activity of writing the book. For example, she satisfied her value of connection by interviewing people rather than researching documents.

COACHING TIPS

Coaching tips

- ✓ Occasionally you may find you are attempting to achieve a goal that doesn't satisfy any of your core values, but facilitates another goal that does. If this is the case, and your motivation is flagging, increase your enthusiasm by reminding yourself that this goal is a stepping-stone to the second goal.
- ✓ Although our values are fairly stable, they can alter, especially if we experience life-changing events or our perspective is shifted significantly. If this has been your recent experience, your values may no longer match some of your goals. This could therefore be a cause of loss of motivation regarding a particular project. If you're reviewing which values link to a particular piece of writing, also check that your values still feel right for you. If they don't, work through Chapter 3 again. If your values have changed significantly, you may need to review all your goals.

FINAL WORD

Motivation is a very personal thing. Choose the methods that work best for you then consider how else you can make them even more personal.

10 THINGS TO REMEMBER

1. Once you have built motivation into your plans and activities, it works silently to maintain interest and enthusiasm with little need for conscious effort.

2. Maintaining good motivation helps creativity flow and is therefore key to preventing potential writing challenges arising.

3. Much of the work you can do in Part one of this book will also build motivation into your writing at a foundation level.

4. Routine and habits might feel like hard work to start with, but they quickly become an invisible part of our motivation strategy.

5. Routines and habits don't just motivate, they also bring you into a more creative frame of mind.

6. Taking time to imagine and get excited about your writing future will increase your motivation to write.

7. Remove negative influences as much as possible, both from external and internal sources.

8. Make sure you take the right type of breaks at sufficiently frequent intervals.

9. Acknowledging achievement is an important motivator.

10. Always ensure the techniques you create to boost and maintain motivation are as personal as possible.

9

Increasing creativity

In this chapter you will learn:
• *techniques to increase creativity.*

What is creativity? We know it relates to originality and imagination and is often connected with artistic endeavours. We know that sometimes people's brains throw up the most amazing ideas in an apparent flash of genius. We know that sometimes we just need to sleep on a problem and in the morning the answer will have arrived in our head.

> ***I dreamed the nightmare sequences to Witch Hill. I was scared.***
>
> **Marcus Sedgwick**

However, we know little about how our creative processes occur. We therefore often see our brains as containing a magic box, usually referred to as the subconscious, that secretly processes ideas then throws out something useful if we're lucky or creative enough.

Yet is there such a thing as a creative person? Clearly some people are more creative than others. But were they born that way? Did something in their upbringing make them that way? Can we all become highly creative, if we train our brains properly? And what about the idea of creative intelligence? Do some of us have a higher 'god-given' CQ than others?

Creativity is an elusive commodity. No one can guarantee that they can come up with a creative idea at the click of the fingers, and it's impossible to measure someone's true creative intelligence – if such a thing exists – because the moment we put people under test conditions, we take away the optimum conditions for being creative. Furthermore, creativity will always remain mysterious and unmeasurable, because unpredictability is one of its defining characteristics.

This chapter, therefore, doesn't claim to scientifically deliver ways of making yourself more creative. It simply aims to discuss how you can create favourable conditions to encourage the 'magic box' in your head to assist you to have a more creative output. It also aims to enable you to put yourself in a place where you are more creative and can discover solutions more easily to move your writing forward in a suitable and original manner.

Accessing the creative state

Creative thinking occurs when we are relaxed and our brains are producing alpha brainwaves. This is a place of deep relaxation, but not quite meditation. In alpha state, we begin to access the wealth of creativity that lies just below our conscious awareness. We often fall into this state when we are doing repetitive, rhythmic tasks that shift our thinking from logical to creative. For example, Einstein is reputed to have complained that many of his ideas came to him in the shower.

> ***When I first started writing seriously I was a bit afraid of the state of intense concentration, and it took time to get used to it. Now, more than two decades later, I can go in and out of it at will, and it's one of my greatest writing tools.***
>
> **L A Weatherly – author**

Theta brainwaves are also responsible for creativity. These are brainwaves that adults normally only experience fleetingly upon waking or drifting off to sleep. In theta state we are in a waking-dream, vivid imagery flashes before the mind's eye and we are receptive to information beyond our normal conscious awareness. Theta brainwaves lead to the flashes of creativity and inspiration we sometimes experience as we are waking up or falling asleep.

RECOGNIZING WHEN YOU ENTER ALPHA STATE

Spend a week observing yourself and note down where and when you have your most creative thoughts. Also note any rhythmic repetitive activities you normally carry out during the week.

Once you have recognized where you naturally lock into creative thought, you can encourage yourself to think about your writing at these times. Focusing on your current writing project, talking to one of your characters or working on your plot are all effective ways of making the most of this space. The key here is relaxation. If you keep thinking that you're looking for the answers you need, you're unlikely to link to your creativity, because these more focused thoughts prevent you from entering alpha state. If you do feel conscious of what you're doing, simply think about your current ideas, putting no attachment on whether you come up with anything useful.

COACHING TIPS

Coaching tips

- ✓ Meditation and relaxation can be used to deliberately bring you into the alpha state. Practising and using these regularly are great tools for getting into your creative zone.
- ✓ Setting a simple reminder of what you are writing about, such as a note to yourself or placing a relevant picture in an appropriate place, can help you remember to think about your writing at the right times.

Insight

Make it a habit to consciously think about your writing at times when you are likely to enter the alpha state or when you recognize that you are in the alpha state. After a while you will automatically focus on your writing at these times without having to make a conscious effort.

Creating original ideas

Most creative outcomes tend to be novel recreations of ideas that already exist. For example, the highly successful young adult *Twilight* series combines teen romance with vampires, while *Harry Potter* is a story of wizards at boarding school. Teen romance, vampires, wizards and boarding school stories were all well-established genres before these series came along, but these combinations were new and exciting.

Note

It's important to also recognize that it's not just the combining of different genres that makes *Twilight* and *Harry Potter* so brilliant.

DEVELOP AN IDEAS POOL

To create novel ideas we need to have a pool of knowledge existing in our minds, which we can draw on to develop new and exciting concepts, right from creating original stories down to developing a fresh simile or metaphor.

The old adage 'write what you know' is a great motto for a writer, yet the assumption is often that what 'we know' is everything we've learned up to this point in our lives. In reality you can know about anything if you care to learn about it. While this is obvious on a logical level, writers can fail to look out for new knowledge unless they are at a point when they are actively seeking fresh ideas. This can unnecessarily reduce our ability to produce original thinking and, if this is the case, we are throwing away a great opportunity to increase our powers of creativity.

If we become generally more curious and make it a habit to regularly learn or experience new things, we will increase the amount of material we have to make new connections both on a conscious and subconscious level. The method set out below will help you find ideas that really excite and engage you.

How curious are you?

If you answer 'no' or 'not very often' to any of the following questions, identify actions you can take to change your answer to a 'yes':

- Do you make time to learn new things?
- Do you take time to learn more about the things that you are curious about?
- Do you visit new places regularly?
- Do you often meet new and different people?
- Do you seek out new experiences?
- Do you browse: leaf through catalogues, newspapers, magazines, surf websites, window-shop, read something you wouldn't normally?

Once you have a list of what to do, take action to bring more of these activities into your life. If you do something new you don't enjoy, still engage, but do it with curiosity. In other words, become intrigued and involved in a way that excites you.

Real life

Mother of four, Michelle, considered how she could become more curious when her life was already so full. She recognized that although she hated how self-centred some of the mothers she met at the school gate were, paying better attention to their conversations, rather than switching off when they talked to her, provided her with a rich seam of comic material for her novel.

CREATE A CURIOSITY NOTEBOOK

After each learning experience you intentionally encounter, note in a separate 'curiosity notebook' the avenues you feel drawn to researching further as a result of the experience.

At the end of each day ask, 'What intrigued me about today?' Note down anything that comes to you.

Make a note of anything you read or hear about, that you think would be interesting to follow up when you have time.

Note

The curiosity notebook is different from the sort of notebook many writers carry around with them to capture images or to flex their writing muscles. A curiosity notebook is for collecting reminders of avenues that interest you and you intend to explore more fully later on.

Using your curiosity notebook

DO use it to:

- identify places you can find new ideas when you are looking to create a new project
- note ideas to explore further
- help you find areas and activities to explore further.

DON'T use it to:

- Write long explanations of what you have done or experienced.
- Force ideas from your experience or learning – leave it for your subconscious to work on what you learn and/or make connections when it is ready.
- Force yourself into experiences or learning you don't enjoy – becoming curious is learning about things that excite you.

ENGAGE MORE FULLY IN EVERY EXPERIENCE

How often do you go to familiar places and really take them in? To what extent do you become engaged in new experiences? Taking time to stop and really experience what is going on will help you build richer learning. This doesn't just apply to intentional learning, but to your everyday life. For example, when you look out the window each morning, how much do you really notice? In future, occasionally take a few moments to really acknowledge what's going on around you. Often interesting things are going on in very ordinary places.

Occasionally, when I'm out and about, I pretend the police are going to ask me to be their key witness later – it's a fun way of making a dull journey more exciting, and means I take in more of the world around me.

Gill Smith – comic and scriptwriter

Coaching tip

Don't forget, engaging fully means switching on all your senses, not just looking:

✓ When you listen to people, don't always think about how what they're saying affects you or how you feel about it. Put yourself in their shoes and consider what it's like to be coming from their point of view.
✓ Listen to the world around you and take in the sounds that you usually are too busy to notice.
✓ If it's not going to get you into trouble or cause harm, touch things out of curiosity.
✓ Consciously take in smells and tastes.

COACHING TIP

MEMORY

Our memories are another curious 'magic box' inside our heads. Much has been learned about them, but there is still much we don't know. However, it's undoubtedly beneficial to our creativity to have a strong memory, to store new learning experiences, in order to make connections and create original ideas.

Many books aimed at improving your memory teach tricks to help you recall things you want to remember. But these techniques are of little help when we want to use memories to generate random ideas and connections. This book, therefore, doesn't teach memory techniques, but gives two suggestions for working to improve your memory:

1 When you have taken on new learning in any form, spend time running it back through your mind or write a summary of what you learned or observed. You're not testing yourself to see if you can remember everything, just working the memories over to embed them more firmly in your brain.
2 Work your memory muscles by playing simple memory games. This follows the general 'if you don't use it, you lose it' strategy – because the more we think of something, the more we strengthen the physical structures in our brain that carry those thoughts.

Memory games

Take five minutes at the end of each day to remember the most interesting thing you learned or the most interesting thing that happened. What else did you learn today?

Take a list when you go shopping, but don't look at it. Challenge yourself to remember everything you need, then check at the end to make sure you didn't miss anything.

If you have children, play memory games with them, such as 'I went to the shops...'. This game is played by the first player saying, 'I went to the shops and bought...', then naming something they bought at the shops beginning with the letter A. (The item can be as unrealistic as you like.) The next player repeats the introduction, then the first player's item plus their own item beginning with the letter B. The next player repeats the introduction then the first player's item, then the second player's item, then their own item beginning with the letter C. The players continue in this fashion working through the alphabet, with the list to remember growing longer and longer until someone can't remember an item previously named.

Electronic games and gadgets often have memory games you can play.

Devise your own games by challenging yourself to remember different things in different situations, such as when you do something new or watch a factual television programme.

CONNECTIONS

Because creativity is about making original connections, we don't just need a pool of knowledge; our brains also need to be good at linking ideas. The following exercise will help encourage your brain to make connections between things you don't normally make associations between.

Connecting the unconnected

This is done by choosing two apparently unconnected items at random when you have a 'bored' five minutes and you're not thinking about your writing, for example, when you're waiting in the supermarket, in the shower, or when you're tidying up. To make the game more challenging, set yourself the task of coming up with ten connections before you get to the checkout, finish your shower, stop tidying etc. If you do this regularly, your brain will become better at making associations between seemingly unrelated concepts. It will also become familiar with making these connections and likely to do it more spontaneously.

CHALLENGE

Challenge – connect the unconnected

Ask yourself what connections you can make between smoke and a gorilla – see the end of this chapter for some possible answers.

Changing perspective

While creating writing routines and habits can be very useful in helping us find creative space and building motivation to write, too many routines and habits can reduce our creativity by keeping our thinking in a rut. Doing things differently and seeing things from different perspectives makes us concentrate harder on what we are doing, encounter new experiences and take in more of what we encounter.

Consider your daily/weekly/monthly/yearly non-writing routines and what you could change about them. For example:

- Can you vary the way you go to work/to the shops/to pick up the kids from school? Think about both the method of getting there and the route you take.
- Do you always exercise in the same manner? Could you vary it more?
- Do you have favourite restaurants/meals/foods? Go somewhere else or have different foods at the restaurants you are familiar with.
- Do you always shop in the same places?
- Do you make an effort to meet new people? What about meeting the type of people who you wouldn't normally associate with?
- Can you gain new physical perspectives by sitting somewhere different, or standing up when you would usually sit down?
- What other routines do you have that you could change?

Insight

Take time to see the world how other people see it. Don't just imagine yourself in others' shoes. Explore other people's art and engage in activities that show you things from another perspective, for example, experiment with a hobby like photography, where the world is seen differently through the eye of a lens.

Divergent thinking

Divergent thinking means looking for more than one answer to a question or more than one solution to a challenge. It is considered to be key to creativity and is a quality often measured in psychometric creativity tests. The main characteristics of divergent thinking are:

- Flexibility – being able to see things from different perspectives.
- Fluency – how quickly someone can come up with different ideas.
- Originality – the uniqueness of an idea.
- Elaboration – the ability to expand an idea beyond what was required by the original challenge or question.

You never really know what your imagination will come up with. I wrote a filler for a magazine called Pet Dogs. It was 100 words. It was a silly idea about why the brand of dog food your dog likes is never the one on offer at the supermarket. It was published and I began thinking about it further.

I expanded the idea into an 800-word article for Dogs Monthly. After that was published, I thought I could take it further still. That article became 100 Ways For A Dog To Train Its Human. Now over 216,000 copies have been printed, and it has a North American, Portuguese and Italian editions!

Simon Whaley

Note

Writers don't just use the characteristics of divergent thinking to come up with original ideas. They also use them within the writing process itself. For example, flexibility is key to understanding writing from different characters' perspectives.

A simple exercise that encourages divergent thinking is to list the number of uses you can think of for an everyday object. For example, a coat hanger could be:

- used to hang clothes
- unbent to make an reception aerial
- unbent and hooked at one end to use as a fishing rod
- wrapped in tinsel and hung as a Christmas decoration
- made into a tent frame for very, very small people or, if it was a giant coat hanger, made into a tent frame for average-sized people or, if it was a gigantic giant coat hanger, made into a tent frame for giants.

Practise divergent thinking by picking everyday objects and identifying how many different uses you could put them to. You will notice this is very much like brainstorming; at first you are likely to think of the more mundane ideas – like hanging your coat on the coat hanger – then practical – creating an aerial – then the more original and bizarre.

Here are a few objects you could think about for starters:

- Coat hanger
- Plant pot
- Fish
- Piece of A4 paper
- Pencil
- Hair band
- Car tyre
- Leaf

Creative attitude

MAINTAIN AN INSPIRED MIND

Ever had the experience of planning to change your car and, having decided what you want, suddenly it seems every other car you see is that type? They aren't really, it's just because once you tell your subconscious you want something, it starts looking for it. This technique can be taken advantage of to help boost your creativity. Just tell yourself you're looking for particular ideas or simply ideas for a story/non-fiction piece and you'll be more likely to notice them. But remember, you'll need to remind yourself what you're looking for every day or your subconscious will stop helping.

BE CREATIVE

Encourage your mind to dwell more regularly in a creative place by taking part in other forms of creativity as often as possible. This doesn't just include artistic endeavours such as drawing, pottery or needlecrafts. It includes being creative in the whole of your life, for example cooking, making jokes and seeking creative solutions for day-to-day challenges.

GET ENOUGH SLEEP

Scientists have proved that getting sufficient sleep is essential to being creative. Ensure that you get your optimum level of sleep each night – for most people this is between six and eight hours.

FINAL WORD: MOOD

When our minds are free from negativity and we're highly motivated, creativity flows more easily. Therefore, working on Chapters 6 and 7 to enhance your positivity, and Chapter 8 to increase your motivation, are also good places to enhance your creative attitude if you haven't worked with them already. Even if you have done the work in Chapters 6 and 7, it's worth considering what further positive thoughts you could add to your thinking which tell you that you are creative or that you are becoming more creative.

However, while divergent thinking is associated with positive mood, reflective thinking, which can also make people more creative, is often a dominant characteristic of negative mood. Therefore, while endeavouring to maintain positivity will aid motivation and creativity, if you are experiencing a negative mood it can enable you to channel your emotions into intense creativity.

CHALLENGE

Challenge – connect the unconnected (answers)

Possible connections between a gorilla and smoke:

- Both can climb to the top of a tree.
- Both are hard to see through.
- Both occur naturally.
- Both are made of carbon atoms.
- Both are/produce emissions that are considered to add to global warming.
- Both are in the title of the film *Gorillas in the Mist*.
- Both have been used in the name of a pop group: Gorillaz and Smokey Robinson and the Miracles.

Self-insight question

When you read the last two answers, did you think they were fine, cheating or a creative interpretation of the question? Use your contemplation journal to discuss what this tells you about your current creative attitude.

10 THINGS TO REMEMBER

1. Creative thinking occurs when you are relaxed and your brain is producing alpha brainwaves.
2. The more you practise shifting into the creative alpha state, the easier it becomes to slip into it.
3. Most creative outcomes tend to be novel recreations of ideas that already exist.
4. Having more knowledge will give you more understanding to make more new connections.
5. Engaging more fully in everyday experiences helps increase creativity.
6. Children's memory games can be a good tool for developing your memory.
7. Increase creativity by practising making connections between apparently unconnected concepts and ideas.
8. Routines can be a great way of building motivation, but don't allow yourself to get into a rut.
9. Practising divergent thinking and being creative foster a creative mind.
10. Positive mood enhances creativity and motivation, but we can be highly creative when we are in a negative mood.

Part three
Challenges

10

Beating procrastination

In this chapter you will learn:
- ***reasons we procrastinate***
- ***ways to stop yourself procrastinating and get on with your writing.***

> ***In a survey of published and unpublished writers, 96% admitted to procrastinating instead of writing.***
>
> The Write Coach

Many writers intend to write, but find themselves carrying out a variety of other activities instead. Procrastination can have many causes and waste a lot of time. However, you may think you are procrastinating when you aren't. What you think is procrastination could be you settling yourself into your writing mindset. This is rather like an athlete stretching, warming up their muscles and mentally pulling themselves 'into the zone' before a race. Your 'procrastination' could therefore be an important part of your creative process.

Are you really procrastinating?

Reflect on the times you procrastinate. Are you collecting and developing ideas or thinking productively in some other way about your writing? Or are you avoiding writing? If you're not sure, next time you think you're procrastinating, stop and consider what you've just been thinking.

Real life

Fifty-six writers were asked what they gained by procrastinating.

Answer	Response per cent*
A solution/thinking time for writing	41%
Nothing	23%
Completed chores	20%
Guilt	13%
Connection to others	9%
A scarier deadline	7%
Frustration	2%
Relief from stress	2%
Avoiding rejection	2%

*Several respondents gave more than one answer.

Cleaning things is always a good way to procrastinate. My house is very tidy.

Marcus Sedgwick

If procrastination is helping nurture your creativity, that's good, unless you're taking a very long time to get to your writing or you're not writing at all. In this case, set yourself a time limit for performing what you previously considered 'procrastination', then sit down and begin writing.

If you struggle to get going, increase the time you 'procrastinate' for. If, after extending this time, you get on with your writing, reduce your 'procrastination' time gradually. Observe the influence that reducing it has on your writing to ensure you don't force yourself to cut your 'procrastination' time too far. It's better to spend a short time writing well, than producing longer pieces of poor quality.

Insight

If you recognize that your procrastination is advantageous to your writing, give these times a new encouraging name, such as musing. This helps reduce feelings of guilt, if you have them, and increases your motivation to write. It will also assist you to distinguish between productive times and true procrastination.

Ten reasons for true procrastination

1 *UNCLEAR PURPOSE OR PLAN*

If we don't give ourselves clear instruction for what we want to achieve, our brains are far less inclined to move us in the right direction and we drift along, because nothing is telling us what to do. A good way to make sure you are consciously and subconsciously focusing on your need to write, is to note down each morning exactly what you want to achieve today as a clear goal.

> ***Knowing exactly what you want allows you to focus more constructively.***
>
> Addy Farmer – children's writer

2 *TOO MUCH TIME*

This is effectively the same as having an unclear plan or purpose. Although we may know exactly what we need or want to do, we haven't told our brain when we're going to do it. To address this, make a specific agreement with yourself what time you're going to start and finish writing and what you're going to do in that time. (Once more, you can create greater impact on your conscious and subconscious thinking by writing it down.) If you find yourself resisting writing at the allotted time, consider what other reasons there are for your lack of motivation.

3 *FEAR*

Sometimes fear fuels procrastination. Often this is linked to the consequences of failure and/or success; if we don't write (or don't submit) we'll never fail or succeed and therefore never have to face the fear(s) that are linked to them.

If you recognize that fear is fuelling your procrastination, think that it might be, or can't find any other reason for procrastinating, go to the section *What are you thinking?* in Chapter 6. However, rather than exploring general negativity about your writing, use Steps 1 to 3 to consider how you would feel if your current writing project:

- failed
- was rejected
- succeeded.

If you identify any fear(s) about success or failure, continue on through Chapters 6 and 7, which will show you how to address, reduce and remove them.

4 *SOMETHING MORE APPEALING IS CALLING YOU*

Almost anything can seem more appealing if there's something you want to avoid. If this is the case, ask yourself, 'What are the reasons this activity is more appealing than my writing?' Also ask, 'What are the reasons my writing isn't appealing to me?' This should identify:

- a challenge you have with your writing that you are avoiding, such as the need to do more research, development or rewriting. If this is the case, decide on an appropriate course of action to overcome the challenge(s) you have identified.
- you're seeing what else you're doing as a higher priority – check that it really is
- you lack interest in your writing – see number 5 in this section: *Lack of interest*
- the other activity really is more enjoyable. If this is the case, ask yourself, 'What are my reasons for continuing to write?' Writing rarely pays well, so if you'd rather be doing something else, then why are you bothering with writing at all?

Note

Some more appealing activities are purely fun and/or addictive, for example computer games. If you recognize this sort of activity is preventing you writing, it is effectively your own thinking that is interrupting you. See number 7 in this section: *Distractions and interruptions*.

> ***My favourite method of procrastination is Spider Solitaire. I also go on Facebook too much.***
>
> Jon Mayhew

5 *LACK OF INTEREST*

If you're not sufficiently interested in what you're writing, ask yourself, 'What are the reasons I'm writing this?' These reasons, or a lack of good reasons, may lead you to decide to move on to another project. If you do, ensure first that the new project is truly of interest to you and fits in with your writing goals. Also, if you know that you have a tendency to get bored part way through a project consider:

- ▶ what you can do to maintain your interest throughout the writing process
- ▶ whether you would be better off working on shorter projects. If you take this course of action, ensure that the strategy fits your writing goals and long-term plans, or that you make acceptable adjustments to them if it doesn't.

Increasing your interest

If you decide to continue with your current project, ask yourself, 'How can I increase my interest in what I'm writing?' Take any appropriate action this question reveals. If you can't think how to increase your interest, brainstorm ideas – Appendix 3 discusses how to carry out effective brainstorming. You may also find it helpful, if you have previously identified your values, to turn to 'Link your goals to your values' in the section *Twenty ways to boost your motivation*, in Chapter 8, and consider how you can use your values to increase your level of motivation.

6 *DEADLINE FOCUS*

Some writers, particularly journalists, enjoy or are so used to writing short deadline-driven pieces, they procrastinate unless they have an impending deadline. If you recognize that deadline focus is causing you to procrastinate, but are happy that you are doing sufficient high-quality writing and hitting your deadlines – there's nothing wrong with it. However, if you feel you need to change this pattern, Chapter 8 can help you build motivation strategies, to make better use of your time and to be more highly motivated well ahead of deadlines.

> ***One of the four writers in the survey, who said they gained a 'scarier' deadline by procrastinating, also said it helped them to focus.***
>
> The Write Coach

7 *DISTRACTIONS AND INTERRUPTIONS*

Most people find it hard to concentrate when they're being distracted by noise or visible movement, or if their own thoughts keep intruding.

Unless you can concentrate with external distractions around you, remove or at least to minimize them as much as possible. If you have disruptive thoughts of the type that encourage you to engage in some pleasant distraction, such as checking your emails, see 'Blocking limiting thoughts', in the section *Taking positive thinking further*, in Chapter 7 to help stop them. But if your thoughts are about concerns you have with your writing or elsewhere in your life, this technique will only be the mental equivalent of sticking your head in the sand – the thoughts, along with whatever is troubling you, will continue to return if you don't deal with them.

Working through Chapters 6 and 7 can help you identify, address and remove negative thinking about your writing, but if your intrusive thoughts are related to the rest of your life, see the later section *Fatigue, stress or poor health*.

The next section, *Ten ways to beat procrastination*, can also help take you away from intrusive thoughts, and Chapter 8 can help you develop motivation techniques to stop yourself getting sucked into other activities when you want to be writing.

> ***My favourite method of procrastination is checking my email.***
>
> Candy Gourlay

Note

Sometimes we keep putting off small undone tasks that relate to other areas of our lives, because they aren't a high priority. When the list of these grows, they nag at us simply because there are so many of them. Even though they aren't important or high priority, it can still be a good idea to occasionally abandon our writing and blitz them, to get them out of the way and stop them causing mental clutter.

8 *FATIGUE, STRESS OR POOR HEALTH*

Sometimes we push on with our writing despite being unwell, stressed or tired. This may be because we have deadlines to meet and have little choice. It may also be because we are passionate about our writing or because we are using writing as an escape from other parts of our lives. If you force yourself to write under these circumstances, mental energy and concentration will be low and your writing is unlikely to be of a good standard. Furthermore, when you are fatigued, stressed or unwell, your priority should be looking after your health and/or addressing the concerns from elsewhere in your life.

9 *INDECISION*

If you can't decide which direction to take within a story, or what to write next in a factual piece, the section *Kick start your writing* in Chapter 12 may be helpful.

If you are struggling to choose between working on different writing projects, go to the section *Making decisions* in Chapter 12.

10 *YOU HAVE A PROCRASTINATION HABIT*

There may be no root cause to your procrastination other than that you have developed a habit of procrastinating. If this is the case, as well as using some of the techniques below, you may find Chapter 8 helpful in building motivation to break the pattern.

Real life

When The Write Coach survey asked, 'What area(s) of writing do you usually put off doing?', the following answers were given:

	Response per cent*
Anything and everything	46%
Continuing a first draft beyond the initial excitement	39%
Rewriting	34%
Submitting	32%
Plotting	23%
Starting a first draft	23%
Character development	18%
Research	9%

*Several respondents gave more than one answer.

Ten ways to beat procrastination

The following motivators are aimed at quickly building inspiration to get you writing when you recognize that you are procrastinating.

1 *MAKE A PACT WITH YOURSELF*

Agree with yourself that you will make a start on your writing and work for just 20 minutes. Once you've started something it often becomes easier to keep going. So if at the end of your 20 minutes you really don't want to continue, stop. But chances are you'll be happy to keep going. If don't want to keep going, check your reasons for procrastinating again and see if you can do more to improve your motivation.

> ***When I don't feel like writing, I make myself write for just 20 minutes. I call these 20-minute writing spells time pockets, which I climb into to write.***
>
> Pamela Johnson – novelist, poet and writing tutor

2 *SET DAILY TARGETS*

If we have a target to aim for, we know exactly what we want to accomplish. So set yourself a daily target in time or words and commend yourself when you achieve it. Having a target to aim for helps you recognize that there is an end to what you're doing. Therefore, if your writing is feeling like a chore, you have the comfort of knowing it won't go on forever. Creating a daily target also breaks your task down into smaller steps which feel more manageable and less overwhelming.

Insight

Some writers I know set a daily quota then post on Facebook when they have accomplished it. Not only does this create a small celebration of their daily achievement, it draws encouragement from their friends.

3 *REFRAME TODAY'S GOAL*

If today's target still seems too much like hard work, break it down even further. Set a realistic goal for what you're going to achieve in the next hour, or even half hour, and reward yourself with a small treat once you've accomplished it. Once you've hit your first target, create a new one for what you'll achieve in the next hour or half hour.

COACHING TIPS

Coaching tips

- ✓ When you work with self-imposed targets, see them as a statement of your intention rather that a rigid deadline to stick to. Don't beat yourself up if you don't achieve them, but don't be too kind either if you allow yourself to get distracted.
- ✓ Keep a check on reality – setting unrealistic targets is setting yourself up for failure.

4 *REVIEW YOUR GOALS*

If you've set goals, reading over them and thinking about what it will feel like when you achieve them and the benefits of achieving them is an excellent way to increase motivation. You could also write down what excites you about achieving any bigger overall goal you're currently working towards and place it somewhere as a reminder of what you're aiming for.

Great places to put reminders of your goals (or inspirational quotes, if they help you) are:

- your purse or wallet
- on your computer monitor
- in your diary
- inside your wardrobe.

Note

Although visual motivators will continue to act as triggers to encourage us to write, after a while we get used to them and have a tendency to ignore what they are telling us. Change them regularly if you want them to remind you to do or think something.

5 *RECONNECT*

When you feel disconnected from a piece of writing, ask yourself:

- What do I want to achieve here?
- What are the reasons this is important to me?
- What are the reasons this is important to others?
- How does this contribute to my longer-term goals?
- How does this fulfil my core values? (You can only answer this question if you have identified your core values in Chapter 3.)

Write your answers down to bring them fully into your awareness.

6 *GIVE YOURSELF A KICK UP THE BUTT*

Sometimes we just need to tell ourselves to stop faffing and putting off and get on with our writing.

> ***I banned myself from the internet one Christmas and had a hugely relaxing and productive couple of weeks!***
>
> Jon Mayhew

7 *POSITIVE SELF-TALK*

Remind yourself why you are working on your current project. When you do this, always:

- ensure you use positive language – see Appendix 2 for an in-depth explanation of positive language
- remind yourself of the benefits of completing this project
- remind yourself of how much you really enjoy writing.

8 *GET EXCITED ABOUT THE NEXT STEP*

New things are usually more exciting, so focusing on the next step you need to take after the one you're working on helps you become excited about the whole project again. If you can't get excited about moving forward with a project, you need to reconsider why you are working on it or what might be stopping you getting excited about it. Once you have identified these things, take appropriate action.

Insight

The bonus of getting excited about the next step is that your subconscious keeps working on it after you've stopped consciously thinking about it and gone back to the part you were working on.

9 *VISUALIZATION AND METAPHORS*

Visualize and get excited about achieving the goal you are working on. Alternatively, create a metaphor for achieving your goal and visualize it. For more information on creating metaphors see the section *Symbolic language: using metaphors to increase success and address your challenges* in Chapter 7.

10 *TAKE REGULAR SHORT BREAKS*

Sometimes, when we're enthusiastic about what we're writing, or pushing too hard to reach a deadline, the sheer intensity of our work leads to frustration and loss of concentration. Chapter 8 discusses taking longer-term breaks to build motivation. However, good quick-fix breaks can take you away from your procrastination when you're sitting at the screen and find your thoughts drifting off.

Ideally you should take regular breaks from the start of your writing period, rather than working so hard you bring yourself to the point where you procrastinate through loss of concentration. However, if you find your concentration keeps slipping, but you don't have time to take a proper break, take a short break that really makes you focus on something else.

When you take short breaks DO:

- leave the room you write in – even better, leave the building
- do something active or relaxing
- engage with the outside world
- engage as fully as possible in what you are doing
- remember, a break only needs to be five minutes long – although, depending on your situation, you may need a longer break.

Coaching tip

COACHING TIP

- ✓ Learn to recognize your concentration limits so that you stop for a break just before you start slowing down.

I write for 45 minutes at a time then take a break. This ensures I'm always writing when my concentration is at its peak.

Pamela Johnson

When you take short breaks, DON'T:

- stay at your desk
- catch up with chores such as making phone calls or answering emails
- spend your break worrying that you are not writing
- keep taking the same sort of short break
- get so engrossed with your break that you don't go back to your writing.

Note

Domestic chores make a good break as they are active. They also allow you to reduce the number of tasks on your household 'to-do' list, which helps you feel generally more in control.

Insight

Internet socializing creates a sense of being connected to others if you're feeling isolated, but it doesn't give you a break from your desk. It can also suck you into wasting a lot of time and become a procrastination habit. Use it as a break with caution!

If you really can't focus

If you really can't find the motivation to write, especially if other concerns are on your mind, it might be best to put your writing away and forget about working on it for a while. Get on and deal with whatever is distracting you, or take the day off if you're just in a rut. However, don't let taking this course of action become a bad habit or an excuse not to write. Also, if you do take the day off, take a break that really nourishes you – see 'Relax, rest and regenerate', in the section *Twenty ways to boost your motivation*, in Chapter 8.

FINAL WORD

Don't forget that building good long-term motivation into your writing life will reduce your chances of slipping into true procrastination.

10 THINGS TO REMEMBER

1. You may think you are procrastinating when in reality you are warming up your writing muscles or working on your writing.
2. Give yourself clear boundaries of when, how long and how much to write.
3. Always ensure that you have sufficient interest in what you are writing.
4. You may work better rushing at the last minute to hit deadlines. If you do, and are happy doing this and are doing sufficient, quality writing, there is no need for concern.
5. Sometimes you just need to tell yourself to get on with your writing.
6. Break down tasks that feel too big into smaller chunks.
7. Place inspiration, such as goals and quotes, where you see it on a daily basis.
8. When you get excited about what you are going to do in the future, your subconscious will work on it after you have stopped thinking about it.
9. Make sure you take the right sort of breaks.
10. Sometimes you just need a morning, afternoon or day off.

11

Finding time to write

In this chapter you will learn:
- *ways to use your time more efficiently*
- *twelve ways to find more time to write*
- *ways to get organized*
- *to identify and deal with five types of people who take your time and energy.*

Time is one commodity we can't make more of, and writing takes up a lot of time. So where do you get more time from when you've already got a busy life and you can't have more than 24 hours in a day?

The trick isn't really about finding more time, but about using your time differently. This chapter will make suggestions and help you recognize ways to use your time in a more efficient manner. However, it's important to remember, when you're changing or adopting new time management strategies, that time management, good or bad, is a habit.

Insight

There will always be more you want to do and more demands from other people than the time you have allows you to attend to.

Consider your current time habits

How much time do you spend reacting to impending deadlines or actions you need to take *now*? Of course we can't always be on top of everything. Domestic dramas such as leaking pipes aren't something we can schedule in and no one pre-plans getting sick. If you've got children, how often do they announce rearranged after-school fixtures with less than 24 hours' notice? And yes, life sometimes does decide to hit us with every predicament it can all at once.

We can't always be in charge, but it's usually less stressful and more conducive to success if we spend the largest proportion of our day making choices; acting to achieve rather than reacting to deadlines or constantly chasing time in order to stay afloat.

However, don't be fooled, good time managers can also be people who are always reacting to events and just hitting deadlines. Some writers, particularly journalists, have to work like this. Others like to work this way. Good time management is not about what you do, but what you choose to do. If you're comfortable with the way you work and the way you use your time, then you are unlikely to have reason to want to change. If you're unhappy and feel your time demands are running your life, then you probably want to find a better way.

ARE YOU CHASING TIME OR IS TIME CHASING YOU?

Give yes/no answers to the following:

- Do you usually achieve what you need to do with ease and time to spare?
- If you only just hit deadlines, do you enjoy this way of operating?
- Do you have time to take up new opportunities as they arise, without squeezing out other important activities or all your leisure time?
- Do you have time to actively seek opportunities?
- Do you have sufficient time to be creative?
- Do you have enough time to write?
- Do you generally feel in control of your time?
- If a minor crisis erupts, do you handle it without experiencing major turmoil?

Once you have answered these questions, take out your contemplation journal and consider:

- How comfortable are you with the way you manage your time?
- What aspects of your time management do you want to change, if any?
- What do you want to achieve with any extra time you create?

If you recognize that you spend your time almost constantly reacting to deadlines and challenges and want to change this, you'll probably need to catch up first. One way you can do this is to decide what you can take a break from and pick up again, once you've got more time to do it. You can also use some of the suggestions in the next section, *Twelve ways to make more time for your writing*, to create more time.

Insight

When you create more time, be careful not to instantly fill the spaces you gain with something new, so you're chasing after deadlines once more.

GET THE GETTING AHEAD HABIT

The following rules can help you make a habit of 'getting ahead' to ensure you use your time well and break the pattern of constantly chasing time.

1 Make it a habit to ask yourself if you really need or want to take on board new activities and projects. Consider:
   - the pros and cons of taking them on board
   - how they align with your goals and current commitments
   - the benefits of pacing yourself more when you start a new activity or project.

2 If you do take on a new project, consider if it needs to be started right now.

3 When you agree to deliver something, check if you are expecting to make the delivery by the skin of your teeth. If you are, where possible, move the delivery date so you have a comfortable margin to respond to any challenges or opportunities that might arise before the deadline.

4 Always leave ten per cent spare time for unexpected occurrences.

5 Ensure that you use the in-built extra time constructively if no opportunities or challenges arise.

CHOOSING NEW HABITS

The most effective way to work out which ideas to adopt from those suggested in this chapter, is to start by looking more closely at the activities you currently spend your time on. Do this by using your contemplation journal to record everything you do in the next week. If the next week isn't going to be a 'typical' week, wait until you can record a 'typical' week. If you never have a 'typical' week, note down regular activities throughout the week and how long they take. Note anything that takes you five minutes or more.

Note

If you have done the work in Chapters 1 to 5, compare how you are spending your time with how you have assigned your priorities to both your writing and your life. This alone may lead you to rearrange the way you use your time.

Insight

Don't be hard on yourself if you're short of writing time because you're giving priority to things that have a higher priority than your writing.

Once you have an overview of your time, consider how you can incorporate the following time-finding solutions into your existing schedule to find more time to write. For any of the actions you decide to adopt, check that you're happy with the potential consequences, particularly if the changes you make affect other people.

Twelve ways to make more time for your writing

1 *REASSIGN AND REMOVE*

Ask yourself which activities are really important to you and your achievements (personal, career or writing). List anything that can be cut from your schedule or delegated to someone else. Cut and delegate as appropriate.

2 *COMBINING ACTIVITIES*

Write a list of activities that could be grouped together, because they use similar resources or take place in the same location. Look at the way your week is structured. What activities is it realistic to combine? Once you've identified them, make a plan to do this.

3 *SLIMMING DOWN*

Consider what you could spread out across the week(s) or do less often. When you do this, remember the importance of having a balanced life. Activities which support your health (for example, exercise) and relationships (for example, meeting up with friends) are often easiest to spread out, but they nourish us and support our writing as well as other areas of our lives. Don't automatically spread activities out because you can, and always reflect on all the possible consequences.

4 *LOSING PERFECTION*

Is there anything you can get away with doing well, rather than brilliantly? If so, use your contemplation journal to ask yourself:

- What are my reasons for doing this brilliantly?

- Do I want to continue doing this so well or is creating more time of greater importance?
- What are the possible consequences if I don't do it as well in future? For example, leaving the dust a day longer can buy you time, but if you're asthmatic, or if you live with an asthmatic, you may be putting writing above good health.

5 *TIME DOWN THE DRAIN*

Make a list of anything you consider you might be taking too long over. Keep a firm grip on reality when you work on this exercise. Be realistic about what you can really cut back on and what actually does take the time it is currently taking. If you recognize that you are lingering over things unnecessarily, consider what reminders you can put in place to ensure that you work more quickly in the future.

6 *DAILY FOCUS*

Focusing on only one project or area each day buys time, because we don't need to keep reconnecting with what we are doing. However, in reality we often work to others' needs and schedules and it's impossible to spend any one day completely focused on one concern. Nevertheless, we can apply this sort of focus to activities we do have a choice over. Choose a theme for the day, such as mopping up outstanding admin, or keep returning to the same writing project. This may not be workable for every day of your life, but even if you only do it on some days, it will allow you to focus on what you want to get done in a more efficient manner.

> ***I've come to think that multi-tasking is over-rated. Trying to do too much at the same time is a recipe for getting nowhere.***
>
> Candy Gourlay

7 *ONE TOUCH*

Introducing a 'one-touch system' for small jobs allows us to manage our time well. Challenge yourself to deal with all you can the first time you pick it up. Putting quick jobs in the 'to-do' pile often doubles the time they take, as we need to refamiliarize ourselves with them the next time we pick them up.

A good place to start practising one touch is with your emails. Don't open and read them unless it's important to find out what they say right now or you're prepared to respond to them immediately. You're likely to spend twice as long on them if you don't.

8 *DOUBLING UP*

One of the bonuses of being a writer is that you can think about your writing while you're doing other tasks that don't require your full attention.

Real life

Consider if there are any other tasks you can double up to create more time for your writing. Single mum Astrid delivered local free papers, because it gave her exercise, some extra money and she could think about her writing while she did it.

9 *MAKE APPOINTMENTS WITH YOURSELF*

We're often so busy working on paying the bills and taking care of the people we love that our writing gets pushed out and ignored. If you have a tendency to do this, make appointments with yourself to work on your writing. Keep them just as you would for a meeting with anyone else. Don't move them unless you really need to. And if you do, reschedule them immediately. It's up to you how long the appointment is for. In reality this is usually a balance between the time you need to get a comfortable amount written and what life allows.

Coaching experience

This is the feedback Dr Sheree Mack – a freelance writer and artist – gave when she set herself three-hour appointments for writing each week.

> ***Just finished the final three-hour slot and it just flew. A change from the beginning of the week when I was thinking, what am I doing? What time am I wasting? And now I'm into the swing of it, I'm enjoying it and thinking I've got so much to do, but I know where to get the time from now!***
>
> After Sheree's first week of making appointments with herself

> ***I have been doing my three-hour sessions this week. I've got one left and I'm doing it after writing this. They have been so inspirational and liberating. I feel that I am achieving***

(Contd)

something while spending my three hours on stories I haven't finished, starting the projects I never thought I would.

After Sheree's second week of making appointments with herself

Insight

Making appointments with yourself is one of the most successful time-finding tools that both my friends and my writing clients have used.

10 *SWITCHING*

An excellent habit for writers to get into is to use switching. This means getting into the habit of switching to thinking about your writing when you do any activity that is conducive to creativity. It can be helpful here to initially set a reminder. For example, place a rubber band on your wrist or put notes to yourself in the places where you do these activities.

Switching can also be very useful if you need to 'warm up' before you start writing. Putting yourself in the right space before you sit down can reduce or eliminate time spent at the keyboard finding the right 'mood'. Do this by setting a trigger of something you do just before you write, such as tidying your desk or making a cup of tea. For more about triggers and how to use them to build motivation, see the section on triggers in *Twenty ways to boost your motivation*, in Chapter 8.

11 *NANOWRIMO*

You may have heard of NANOWRIMO (National Novel Writing Month). Those taking part set a goal of writing a novel in a month. (Although, of course, you can set a goal to write a non-fiction book or script in a month instead.) NANOWRIMO has the same effect as appointments. It makes you sit down and get on with it. A lot of people who do this realize how much writing they can fit into their busy lives and that it's not such a daunting task to produce a large piece of work. They often also learn a great deal about their writing as well as the use of their time.

There is also the more recently evolved Picture Book Marathon, which is a similar motivational tool, where children's writers are encouraged to write 26 picture books in a month.

If you are interested in taking part in NANOWRIMO or the Picture Book Marathon, details can be found in *Taking it further* at the end of this book.

12 *GRAB WHATEVER TIME YOU CAN*

You may have considered your week fully and attempted to rearrange it, yet still find your time is in short supply. If this is your challenge, have a go at developing the habit of snatching time whenever you can – working on your writing for a total of just one hour each day adds up to nine 40-hour weeks every year.

To make this time as productive as possible don't worry about making your writing perfect. Just get down what you can. Review and revise later. If you have trouble picking up from where you left off, make a note when you stop to remind yourself what you need to write next time. Also set an alarm or a timer so you don't break your focus or waste any precious seconds checking the clock.

> ***When my children were babies, I usually wrote in 5–20 minute gaps every few days – but it's amazing how productive those times can be when they're so few and far between.***
>
> Juliet Clare Bell – children's author

Get more organized

LISTS

Lists are great for making effective use of our time and ensuring we don't forget to do certain jobs, but the way we make and use them can have an enormous impact on their effectiveness.

> ***I use lists to 'park' things that I need to remember, or I'm worried about, so I come back to them later. It frees up time and energy in my head to concentrate on the task at hand rather than juggling, or flitting between things and never settling.***
>
> Benjamin Scott – freelance writer

Creating and using to-do lists

1. Use a pad of paper to write your list on – odd scraps of paper get lost too easily.
2. Some people find it useful to have different lists for different types of jobs.
3. Keep your list close at hand so you can add to it when jobs occur to you.

4. Group similar jobs together, such as telephone calls, and jobs that you do in the same place. That way you're more likely to work on them as a group and save time.
5. Assign priorities to every job on the list and stick to them.
6. Tackling jobs you don't want to do or don't enjoy first is usually more satisfying and more motivational, because your list becomes 'easier' once they're done.
7. Don't just note what you're going to do, note exactly what you're going to do and by when. A to-do list is really a goals-for-the-day list. Making today's goals as clear as possible makes them more achievable.
8. Make following your list more fun by challenging yourself to complete the minor tasks, or a particular set of jobs, as quickly as possible. But don't be in such a hurry that you risk injuring yourself or others.
9. Make a 'to-do later' list if you know you can't do something today. It's far more motivating to complete your daily list each day than to transfer one or more jobs onto tomorrow's list – especially if you ignore the same job(s) day after day.
10. If you find yourself constantly moving a job onto the 'to-do later' list, ask yourself, 'What's stopping me completing this?' The answer will either confirm that the job is very low priority, something you need to abandon, or it will raise other issues you need to address. If you continually put off the same low-priority tasks, have an occasional blitz. Even if they are on the 'to-do later' list, their constant presence will drain your energy.
11. Savour the moment every time you tick off or put a line through something on your list – especially when you complete the final task.

A list gives a working day a clear shape: a beginning and, most importantly, an end – you don't feel like you're on an interminable treadmill.

Candy Gourlay

ORGANIZING YOUR SPACE

When disorder gets out of hand we can waste a lot of time working around our mess and hunting for notes and research that has got lost beneath it. Nevertheless, organizing your space can be a fine balance for writers, if we believe creativity thrives in chaos and find too much order stifles our muse.

If you believe being tidy will erode your creativity, it probably will. Complete the following sentences five times each, in your contemplation journal, to see how you feel:

- Being organized means...
- Organized people are...
- To be creative I need to be...

If you recognize any answers you come up with as beliefs that are holding you back in any way, go to Chapter 6, which explains how what we think and believe has a greater impact on our success than we often give it credit for. It also explains how you can reduce that impact.

GETTING ORGANIZED

- Don't just deal with the obvious mess that's holding you up. Clear the hidden clutter in untidy cupboards and drawers too.
- If you really hate tidying up, get a friend to help or make a game or challenge of getting organized. But don't forget, if you get a friend to help, you may well have to spend time returning the favour.
- If you can afford it, always keep a spare of anything that gets used up or worn out quickly, particularly the things you use to write, but also anything else. Every time you open the spare, put that item on your shopping list. That way you always have that item to hand when you need it and don't have to head out to the shops during time designated for writing.
- If you don't operate a shopping list, create one and put it where you'll always find it.
- Being organized includes regularly backing up your writing.
- Ask yourself how you're going to stay organized in the future and identify systems or routines to stay organized.

Five people who take up your time and how to deal with them

Other people have a big impact on our lives. Consider the following and any changes you can make relating to them. However, as you do, bear in mind that usually it's the people we love that are taking our time and that's often fine, because they are usually our highest priority.

1 *MESSY PUPS*

Consider who is slowing you down by:

- making a mess and expecting you to tidy it up
- losing your stuff
- making a mess and disrupting your calm and smooth energy flow.

Consider how you can address these messy pups, then get on and deal with them.

COACHING TIPS

Coaching tips

- ✓ Messy pups need to be considered realistically. Most two year olds can't understand the meaning of tidy, let alone why you want it that way.
- ✓ If others' mess isn't impacting on you, then leave it for them to tidy up.
- ✓ Don't underestimate older children's ability to be tidy or to tidy up.
- ✓ Tidiness isn't worth starting a war over. Always consider who you're dealing with and take the smartest option.

2 *PEOPLE YOU SAY 'YES' TO WHEN YOU MEAN 'NO'*

Write a list in your contemplation journal of anyone or anything you automatically say 'yes' to, when you could say 'no'. Also add the people or activities you would like to say 'no' to, but:

- are too afraid to
- are too polite to
- don't want to let down
- you feel you're the only one who can help them.

When you've made your list, choose one person or activity that you want to say 'no' to. Resolve to say politely, but firmly, 'no' next time they ask you to do something.

Once you have said 'no' once, consider who else you can say 'no' to and make your way through your list.

COACHING TIPS

Coaching tips

- ✓ Keep observing yourself when you respond to other people. Are there other times you say 'yes', but mean or want to say 'no'?
- ✓ Learning to say 'no' can be quite daunting, but once we start, it does become easier.

- ✓ Choose softer areas to say 'no' to at the start and build up to the more challenging. Also be aware, you may become good at saying 'no' in certain circumstances but not in others.
- ✓ Don't stop half way – keep working on saying 'no' until you are only saying 'yes' when you really mean 'yes'.

3 *PEOPLE WHO OVERSTEP YOUR BOUNDARIES*

Who regularly interrupts you when you're writing or attempting to do other work? Make a list in your contemplation journal of who they are and identify what boundaries you want to draw for them. Explain your boundaries and ask them to respect them.

Coaching tips

- ✓ Children usually need telling about your boundaries more than once. Be persistent, work on their level and explain things in the way they see them. Let younger children feel involved, for example, by making a 'do not disturb sign' or asking them to time 20 minutes for you to work so they can come and tell you to stop.
- ✓ Consider how you can influence interruptions. For example, if are you irresistibly drawn to the phone ringing, unplug it, switch it off, or turn the sound off. If you get sucked into the internet, ban yourself from using it until you have finished writing for the day. If you still can't resist, take yourself somewhere you can't get a connection.

COACHING TIPS

4 *ARE YOU A WORK HORSE OR A WRITER?*

Friends, husbands, wives, children, siblings and parents often need our help and support in their endeavours. Use your contemplation journal to consider who you support and think about where you are putting your priorities.

Of course you want to support the people you love. But at what cost? Are you doing all the giving? Could these people be more respectful of your ambitions? Do you really need to do all you do for them? If you do, fair enough. If not, consider how you can reduce what you do, or stop altogether, without the consequences being unacceptable to you.

Only you know the answers about what you do for any one individual. So only you can work out how to minimize their influence without removing the support you want to give or damaging your relationship with them. If you want to withdraw some or all of your support, consider what you can say to achieve a positive reaction rather than a negative one.

> ***One thing I've been doing for years is a swap where I take a friend's children after school one day a week and the next week, she takes mine. And on alternate weeks, I do it with another friend: it's an extra 2½ hours' writing time each week and my children get to spend extra time with their friends.***
>
> Juliet Clare Bell

You can also go a step further here and actively enlist your loved one's support. Ask them to help you by gently reminding you that you are meant to be writing when they see you procrastinating or getting distracted.

Insight

It's easy to be coy about your writing, especially when you first start. Make sure you let your loved ones know how important your writing aspirations are to you, so they respect the time and space you need to work on them.

Beware

Supporting others can also be a ploy to put off writing.

If you spend any part of your life supporting, nurturing or caring for others, take out your contemplation journal and ask yourself, 'Am I using my responsibilities as a procrastination tool?' When you consider this question, remember that both real and imaginary needs for support may be holding you back. Ensure that you consider each thread of your situation carefully.

If you discover that procrastination is influencing you here, take a look at Chapter 10 to consider procrastination further. You may also find Chapter 8 on boosting motivation helpful in breaking this habit.

> ***I'm really good at putting things for other people ahead of my own work. I'm always checking emails to see if other people need things, then procrastinating by replying to them and going way beyond what I should be doing for them.***
>
> Benjamin Scott

5 *BLOOD SUCKERS*

Some people take from us (intentionally and unintentionally) without ever giving something back. We put up with it because we accept that's the sort of person they are.

Take out your contemplation journal and consider who:

- only shows up in your life when they want something from you
- is overly critical and gets you stressed out or feeling negative about yourself
- has such a negative outlook it drags you into their turmoil, takes up your time and reduces your connection with your creativity.

Next, use your journal to contemplate:

- the reasons you allow them into your life
- if you really want them to remain in your life
- if it's time you made some new friends
- if they're someone you can't or don't want to lose from your life, how you can reduce their negative impact.

As you consider these questions remember, as with the previous exercises, your decisions will be dependent on:

- what/who you're dealing with
- circumstances
- the potential consequences.

Coaching tip

COACHING TIP

✓ You don't have to fire people from your life at enormous velocity. Slowly cutting ties can be a lot more practical and usually less painful.

ADDRESSING PEOPLE WHO TAKE UP YOUR TIME

Relationships are important and complex. Any time you decide to make changes to a relationship, ask:

- What are the possible consequences of taking this action?
- What are the possible consequences of not taking this action?
- What do I really want to do?
- What am I going to do?

Once you have decided what to do, you need to be happy to take responsibility for all the possible consequences.

Make good time management a habit

Replacing old habits with new ones and making them second nature takes a while. Don't change too much too quickly. The following approach works best whatever new time habits you choose to adopt and when forming any new habit:

- Identify what habit(s) you want to change.
- Choose one new way of working that appeals to you.
- Decide how you're going to implement this as a habit in your life.
- Check that there are no obvious reasons why it won't work within your current situation.
- Ensure that you are happy with any potential consequences of adopting this habit, both for yourself and others.
- Choose how you're going to remind yourself to work this way until the method becomes second nature.
- Work with your chosen method until it becomes an unconscious habit.
- Check that the new habit is having its intended impact.
- Take on board another new habit, if you want to.

FINAL WORD

As you work on bringing new time management strategies into your life, you might feel like you're using more time building this new way of being than you're gaining. You may be, but once you get the hang of them, you will save time. The extra time you spend at the start is an investment in your future.

Also remember, however much writing you get done, doing some is better than doing none, because if you don't write, you'll never be a writer.

10 THINGS TO REMEMBER

1. The key to good time management is prioritizing and using your time effectively.

2. Good or bad, time management is a habit.

3. There will never be enough time to be doing everything you want to do.

4. Good time managers can be people who react to events and just hit deadlines as well as those who work well ahead of themselves.

5. If all else fails, grab whatever time you can.

6. Don't be hard on yourself if you're short of writing time because you're giving priority to things that have a higher priority than your writing.

7. Don't bring too many new time management strategies into your life in one go.

8. Make sure you let your loved ones know how important your writing aspirations are to you.

9. Always check how the changes you make influence the rest of your life and those around you.

10. If you don't find time to write, you'll never be a writer.

12

When the words don't flow

In this chapter you will learn:

- *techniques to free your writing when you feel stuck or unable to write*
- *steps to take when you believe everything you write is coming out wrong*
- *how to connect to your next book/script when you're struggling to get started*
- *what to do when you feel overwhelmed by a large project*
- *to find direction when you don't know which project to work on.*

There are times for all writers when the words don't flow. Sometimes they see this as part of their process: stopping to plot because they don't know where they're going; researching more deeply; developing characters further; taking a break to gain mental space; dealing with something else in life; recognizing their personal rhythms aren't currently favourable to writing. Other times writers see the periods when words don't flow as being blocked or suffering from writer's block; experiencing an inability to write certain stories, write any story, or, in the extreme, even to write a shopping list.

What is writer's block?

Writer's block is often talked about as if it is some special clogged-up state that writers become unwillingly engulfed in, akin to catching a debilitating disease. However, when a survey, carried out by The Write Coach, asked writers what they believed writer's block to be, explanations fell into the following categories:

- laziness, excuses not to write, procrastination, lack of enthusiasm
- life getting in the way, external stresses

- insufficient research, plotting, dissatisfaction with a piece of writing
- lack of confidence, low self-esteem, fear of failure, fear of success
- depression
- lack of inspiration, mind seizing up.

Although 66% of respondents said they had experienced writer's block – some for periods of longer than a year – almost all came up with a tangible explanation that both identified the cause for not writing and provided the solution to get going again. It might have been true their writing wasn't flowing, but it wasn't because they had a particular condition that stopped them. Their inability to write was caused by varying explanations, such as they lacked confidence, hadn't done sufficient groundwork, were stressed, or didn't want to rewrite a piece they had already written. Only 16% attributed not writing to their mind seizing up or lacking inspiration and none of these respondents expanded their definition further to indicate if they thought anything tangible had contributed or not.

Why it's dangerous to tell yourself you've got writer's block

Although you may know on a logical level that writer's block isn't a special state, you can still slow yourself down just by thinking or saying you have writer's block. You also reinforce the way you feel, because our brains work in a way that if we believe something, it becomes harder for us to act against it (see Chapter 7). Therefore believing we are blocked or have writer's block will make us more likely to get stuck in the future and less able to move forward once we are struggling to make our words flow.

Challenge – self-insight

Note down in your contemplation journal, or just on a scrap of paper, what the words 'block' or 'blocked' mean to you – write the sort of description that you would expect to find in a dictionary.

Read back over your definition. What feeling(s) does the word 'block' or 'blocked', give you? What picture(s) spring to mind? If you say, 'I have writer's block' or, 'I am blocked', these are likely to be the sort images and feelings it generates.

CHALLENGE

A good start to removing 'blocks' is therefore not to think or say that you have writer's block. In future, if you hear yourself saying or thinking you are blocked, or have writer's block, stop and remind yourself that you are currently working out how to move your writing forward, or use some other positive wording.

Of course, if you don't believe writer's block exists that's a great start, because your lack of belief means that you will never label yourself as having writer's block.

Note

Phrases such as 'I am stuck' or 'I can't make a decision' will also have a similar negative influence on our ability to move forward. Chapters 6 and 7 explain in greater detail how we limit ourselves by what we think and say. They also explore how to identify and reduce detrimental language. If you haven't worked through Chapters 6 and 7, you may find them very helpful if you are someone who experiences low motivation or 'blocks'.

Freeing up your writing muscles

Eradicating the word 'block' from our vocabulary isn't a magic wand. Creativity and the ability to put the words down on the paper will always ebb and flow. There will always be times when we find ourselves wondering how to move our story forward or when we are displeased with what we are writing.

If that's the place you're in right now, ask yourself, 'What's stopping me writing the piece I want to work on?' Spend a few minutes writing the answers that come to you in your contemplation journal. Don't just think about the areas identified in the survey mentioned earlier, consider what's stopping you personally from writing.

COACHING TIP

Coaching tip

✓ Ask yourself the question three times after you think you have come up with all the answers you can find, just to make sure you've found all the reasons.

Some answers may lead you to know immediately what is stopping you and what action to take. You may, therefore, not wish to continue with this chapter any further. For example, you may decide to take action relating to your writing, such as doing more research or plotting. It could also mean leaving your writing for now and paying more attention to other parts of your life.

If you don't immediately decide on a course of action, consider which of the following challenges fit what you have identified most closely:

- **a** You have started writing something, or want to start writing, but are 'stuck'.
- **b** You are dissatisfied with everything you write.
- **c** You are struggling to connect/get going with a new writing project.
- **d** You feel daunted or overwhelmed by the size of the project you want to tackle.
- **e** You can't decide which project to work on.
- **f** When you sit down to write, or think about writing, you feel a sense of fear or panic and/or your head fills with thoughts such as: 'I can't do it', 'It'll never be good enough', 'Why am I wasting my time?', 'Last time was just a fluke', 'I don't know enough about it', 'No one will ever publish it.'
- **g** Your motivation is low.
- **h** You lack creativity.
- **i** You are procrastinating.
- **j** Your lack of flow has been prompted by receiving a rejection.

If you answered:

- **a** Go to the section *Kick start your writing* in this chapter.
- **b** Go to the section *When you are dissatisfied with everything you write* in this chapter.
- **c** Go to the section *Connecting to a new project* in this chapter.
- **d** Go to the section *Feeling daunted or overwhelmed* in this chapter.
- **e** Go to the section *Making decisions* in this chapter.
- **f** Go to Chapter 6 and use the exercises there to fully identify and address the thoughts you are having. Chapter 7 can also help eradicate these thoughts once you have a plan to deal with them.
- **g** Chapter 8 can help you work on your motivation.
- **h** Chapter 9 can help you work on re-energizing your creativity.
- **i** Take a look at Chapter 10, which addresses the causes of procrastination and offers some suggestions to overcome it.
- **j** Chapter 13 can help you to address your reaction to rejection.

However, before you begin to work on your challenge, consider putting your subconscious on the case.

Employ your subconscious

METAPHORS

Employ your subconscious to act silently against your challenges by creating and visualizing a metaphor that describes you overcoming them. The section *Symbolic language: using metaphors to increase success and address your challenges* in Chapter 7 explains this technique and gives examples.

SLEEP ON IT

You can also set your subconscious to work at night by asking it to find a solution to your challenge before you go to sleep. Taking this course of action may lead you to have a dream that helps you move forward, or you may find some of the answers come to you on waking.

> ***That moment when you suddenly resolve a problem you've had with a plotline is electrifying. Suddenly, everything seems possible, and nine times out of ten, these moments happen in the middle of the night!***
>
> Simon Whaley

Even if you wake feeling you have moved no further forward, work calmly on your challenge when you are ready. Having let your subconscious contemplate overnight should still have assisted your thinking.

Note

Gaining benefit from 'sleeping on it' usually requires some conscious consideration before our silent mind can behave in this way. So this technique isn't just about asking your sleeping brain to find the answers to a challenge, you need to spend time first consciously considering what your solutions could be. Since you are reading this chapter, you've probably done that already for your current concerns. However, in future, remember that if you want to find a solution to a challenge you need to give it some conscious thought, before your subconscious is able to help out.

Sleeping on it really does work

Research participants were shown a mathematical problem that required a creative solution before sleeping through the night for eight hours. In the morning they did better at solving the problem than those who were not allowed to read through it before they went to sleep.

Kick start your writing

This section provides a selection of exercises to get you writing. Some may have more appeal or ability to free you up than others, depending where you are in your creative process. Read through them all and decide on the most suitable.

1 *CONSIDER IF YOU'VE DONE ENOUGH GROUNDWORK*

Ask yourself how fully you have developed your ideas. Would doing more basic exploratory work help, such as more thorough plotting, character development or research? You could also focus more specifically on asking questions about the piece by doing Exercise 4 *Interrogation*, which follows later.

If you truly believe you have made sufficient conscious effort, then you probably simply need to allow yourself some downtime for your subconscious to process it further, before you think about it again. However, this doesn't mean you can't work on your writing in some other way while you allow this to happen. Exercises 3 *Skip a bit* and 5 *Read your way out of it* offer activities which you can work on.

> ***I always have a few stages I go through with writing a new book. First I'm wildly enthusiastic and start writing straight away. Then I get to about 5000 words and grind to a halt, full of doubt, and realize that I need to map the story out very carefully and get to know my characters better.***
>
> Jon Mayhew

2 *WRITE YOUR WAY OUT OF IT*

Sit down and write the next part (or the start) of your story/non-fiction. Keep writing for 20 minutes however bad your ideas or your writing seem to be. Starting the writing act itself can help loosen up your thinking and writing muscles.

If you struggle through the whole 20 minutes being plagued by thoughts that you can't write, or by any negativity about your writing or the story itself, take a look at Chapters 6 and 7. These will help you understand the roots of the negativity that your internal thoughts are voicing. It will also help you fully recognize and address the limiting thinking that is stopping your words from flowing.

3 *SKIP A BIT*

If you know what happens later on in your story then skip over the part you can't get right and work on a section or chapter that comes later. When you come back to the skipped section, chances are you'll have freed yourself up to write it.

Insight

Unless there are structural challenges with your work, ensuring that you keep your motivation and creativity high can prevent you from getting stuck in the first place.

4 *INTERROGATION*

Use your contemplation journal to discuss with yourself any of the following questions that apply to what you're working on:

- What could have happened earlier in the piece to make it more interesting/funny/challenging?
- What do I want to change/add/take away?
- What could have happened earlier to make this more like the story I first thought I was writing?
- Are all my characters working as hard as they could be?
- Is there sufficient conflict?
- What's the worst thing that could happen to the protagonist right now? *List six options.*
- What's the best thing that could happen to the protagonist right now? *List six options.*
- Where does this need to go next? *Write a list.*
- Where could this go next? *Write a list.*

Identify from your answers either:

- a key thread you need to change
- an isolated part you want to change
- the direction you want to head in.

Start writing, making the necessary changes or taking the piece forward in the way you consider best.

The most important thing with this method is to take action and see where it leads. Have a go at something different if the first action doesn't work out. When you take just one small step to improve what you have done then you know you can take another and another...

Beware

Keep all your old drafts in case you decide you don't like the changes you've made.

5 *READ YOUR WAY OUT OF IT*

Do one, some or all of the following:

- Read advice on writing or about other authors' ways of working. Consider if any of this would work for you.
- Research factual areas of your story more extensively. This can help you find new paths, or simply reconnect you to your original enthusiasm.
- Read fiction of the same genre and reflect on what makes it work and what doesn't.
- Read for enjoyment to get you back into the flow.

6 *GIVE IT A REST*

Put your writing away and forget about it for a couple of weeks. Write something else or take a complete break. If your mind wanders back to your work, allow it to, but remain detached from whether this thinking produces a way forward or not. Even if you don't stumble on any insights during your 'time off', returning with a fresh eye should help revive your enthusiasm.

> ***I have several projects on the go at any one time (article, short story, non-fiction book, novel) so there's always something I can work on if I find something isn't flowing well on another project.***
>
> Simon Whaley

7 *MOOD*

When your words aren't flowing as smoothly as you'd like them to, check if anything in your life is impacting on the way you feel. Consider everything: relationships, environment, hormones, even the weather. Identify steps you can take to remove or reduce this influence.

Note

If you have concerns about a story itself, you may find a writing class, tutor or a critique group is of help in addressing why your writing isn't progressing as you'd like it to.

When you are dissatisfied with everything you write

We are usually dissatisfied with our writing for one of two reasons:

- because we don't like the writing itself and don't believe it's good enough
- because we don't like the content of what we are writing.

IF YOUR WRITING ISN'T GOOD ENOUGH

If you think everything you write is no good, work on this challenge by writing for 20 minutes, refusing to allow your internal voice to comment negatively. Simply stop the thoughts each time you hear them and tell them you're not listening and you don't care what your writing's like, you're simply writing.

You may find that your writing begins to flow more satisfactorily within this time. If it does, keep going. If it doesn't, when you've finished, look back through what you've written and only allow yourself to comment positively. If you can't find anything positive about the piece, identify what you need to do to improve it and take action to improve your skill in that area. Also, if you can't find anything positive to say, get some objective feedback on your work to identify where you're being too hard on yourself and where there is room for improvement.

Note

Objective feedback is rarely gained from family or friends under any circumstances. If they know you're unhappy with your writing, they're even less likely to be objective, because they'll want to make you to feel better. Kindness might make you happier in the short-term, but it won't help you identify your work's true merits or areas for improvement.

> ***If I thought too much about the blank page then I wouldn't put pen to paper or fingers on keys. I think I know what I write first is going to be crap, but I know the gems will come eventually if I just keep going.***
>
> Dr Sheree Mack

Consider if your mood is influencing you
When we're in a low mood our focus becomes narrower and we are likely to explore what we're considering more deeply. Inevitably this will mean we are more critical of our work when we are in a negative frame of mind. Don't allow your mood to overshadow the realities of your writing abilities. Addressing what's bringing you down may be the real route to improving the way you feel about your writing.

IF YOU DON'T LIKE WHAT YOU'RE WRITING

If you're unhappy with the content of your writing consider the following:

1 Are you avoiding further research, development or rewriting?
If this is the case, the only answer is to get on and do some more research, development or rewriting.

Note
Exercises 1 *Consider if you've done enough groundwork* and 4 *Interrogation* in the section, *Kick start your writing* earlier, may be of help if you need to do more research or development.

2 Are you rushing your creative process?
Sometimes we need to give more time to consciously mulling our work over and/or allowing our creative juices to stew in our subconscious, before we can produce a satisfactory piece of work.

Note
Exercises 3 *Skip a bit* and 5 *Read your way out of it*, in the section *Kick start your writing* earlier, will allow you to continue working on your writing while your thoughts grow. Alternatively, you can work on something else or take a break. For more on taking breaks see 'Rest, relax and regenerate' in the section *Twenty ways to boost your motivation* in Chapter 8 and 'Take regular short breaks' in the section *Ten ways to beat procrastination* in Chapter 10.

3 Have you become disconnected from your work, or lost sight of your original goal for the project?
If this is the case, ask yourself:

- What did I originally want to achieve? *If you're just starting, ask,* What do I want to achieve?
- What are the reasons this is important to me?

- What are the reasons this is important to others?
- How does this contribute to my long-term goals?

Does identifying answers to these questions show you how you can take the piece forward more satisfactorily? If not, and you have identified your values in Chapter 3, use the following method to consider if the solution to your challenge is connected to your values.

Considering your writing's connection to your values

If you've become disenchanted with what you're writing, it may be because:

- You've chased off after an exciting idea that didn't connect strongly enough to your values in the first place. In this case you're likely to be dissatisfied with a lot of what you've written or the whole project itself. If you feel this way, check how many of your core values are satisfied by the project. If a piece of writing isn't strongly connected to your values, consider if you can connect more values to it, change it to fit more of your values, or if you want to abandon it.
- The piece you are writing has evolved into something different to what you originally thought it was and has become disconnected from some of the values that it originally connected to. For example, you may have started writing a suspenseful ghost story, which satisfied a value of intellect, but have veered off into horror. In this case you are likely to only be dissatisfied with some of what you have written. If you like some parts of what you have written, but not others, ask yourself, 'Do these different parts satisfy different values?' Also ask, 'What values do I want this the piece to fulfil?' and 'How can I achieve this?'
- Your core values have changed significantly. If the two comparisons above don't lead you to recognise a way forward, reflect on your core values to check that you still see them all as deeply important. Also consider whether you have had any experiences that have significantly changed your perspective or understanding since you identified your core values. If you have, how has this influenced them? Could you now no longer want to write what you are writing? If you're unsure, repeat the relevant exercises in Chapter 3 to check if your values have changed significantly.

Note

If your core values have changed significantly, you may not only find that you are not longer satisfied by the type of writing you previously enjoyed. You may also discover that writing itself has become a lower priority or you might not want to continue writing at all. If you are seriously questioning your writing ambitions, use Chapter 1 to reflect on what you want to achieve both with your writing and in the rest of your life.

Connecting to a new project

Whether we like it or not, we have a relationship with our writing. When we move on to a new book or script, we move on to a new relationship and our feelings about it are always coloured by the relationships we've had with our previous writing projects.

STARTING YOUR NEW RELATIONSHIP

If you are struggling to get a new book or script started, reflect on the fact that you are leaving a relationship behind and beginning a new, at least partially, unknown one. Take out your contemplation journal and ask yourself the following questions about the project you have just finished:

- What challenges did I encounter?
- What did I hate or dislike about the piece itself or about working on it?
- What did I find easy?
- What did I love about the piece or enjoy about working on it?

Then ask:

- How is my past experience influencing my apprehension to move forward? Don't just consider what your answers to the above questions reveal. Also consider if you hold concerns from before you started the last piece.
- What are my fears?
- Do I have any general fears that could be influencing my apprehension to move forward?

When you answer the last three questions, keep looking for more reasons for your stagnation. Even after you think you've found the last answer to each of the questions, ask the question again.

Often the deepest truths and worst fears are hidden behind all the others.

Insight

Positive experiences can throw up fears as well as negative experiences. Fears about not achieving what we achieved before can be as real and debilitating as being afraid of repeating an unhappy experience.

Once you have identified the reasons contributing to your lack of connection, identify how you can eliminate them, so they allow you to connect to your new piece of writing. If you struggle to do this, work through the section *What's stopping you?* in Chapter 6, considering each reason you have identified as something that is 'stopping you'. Also recognize that the previous piece you wrote was a learning experience and use the following section to incorporate that learning in your next project.

LEARNING FROM THE PAST

Write your answers to the following questions in your contemplation journal.

- How has my writing improved from the experience of writing the previous book/script?
- How have I grown from the experience of writing the previous book/script?
- What obstacles did I overcome to write last my book/script?
- What did I learn about my writing?
- What did I learn about myself as a person?
- What did I learn from others?
- How will I take this learning forward into writing the next book/script?

For anything that makes you feel you 'failed', ask the following extra questions:

- What didn't work out as I planned or hoped it would?
- What are the reasons it didn't work out?
- What could I have done differently so I did get the result I was looking for?
- What have I learned?
- How will I take this learning forward into writing the next book/script?

ADDRESSING YOUR ATTITUDE FURTHER

Let go of the past

If you've been struggling to let go of fears generated by writing your previous book or script, consider how you can mentally 'let it go'. Just like old lovers, the more we think about writing projects we have worked on before, the more they haunt us. That's fine if they're telling you something positive, but not if they're slowing you down.

If the fear associated with your past experience(s) are purely negative echoes within your thinking, work through Chapter 7 from the start of the section *Taking positive thinking further*. The exercises in this chapter will show you how to remove the thoughts that are holding you back. However, if your fears are grounded in possible realities, ask yourself, 'What can I do to ensure this fear does not become a reality?' – If you struggle to find an answer to this question, Appendix 3 gives guidance on how to perform effective brainstorming.

Once you have found a solution to the question above, use the section *Taking action against thoughts that limit success*, in Chapter 6, to formulate a goal and action plan to deal with this. You may also find it helps to read the section *Fear, apprehension and lack of confidence* that precedes this.

You can also mentally let go by simply telling yourself that you are letting go, creating and visualizing a metaphor for letting go – see the section *Using metaphors to address your challenges* in Chapter 7 – or carrying out a symbolic action of your own choosing.

Note

If you think fondly of your previous work, you may wish to mentally thank it for teaching you and tell it that you will be remembering it by using what you have learned from it in the future.

Connect with your new project

As you move forward, tell yourself the positives about your new book/script. Remind yourself that you can't instantly know your subject, characters or plot as well as you know them in the previous book or script. Allow yourself time to learn about your new subject or story and for your creative processes to work on it. You can also create a metaphor of how you see the project as a whole or how you want your journey of working on it to be. See the section

Symbolic language: using metaphors to increase success and address your challenges in Chapter 7.

The blank page

Hopefully you're now ready to write. However, if you're still feeling apprehensive about making future mistakes, open a new document (or take out a new piece of paper if you write your first draft longhand), take a deep breath and start to write. Go for it. Make a mistake. Once you've smudged the paper it doesn't matter so much that you make another smudge. Keep working at getting it right, because in truth you have two alternatives: write your next project or don't. It's entirely up to you which option you choose.

> ***The only failure is the failure to write.***
>
> Pamela Johnson

Feeling daunted or overwhelmed

Writers often struggle with larger projects such as books or scripts because:

- they don't know how to structure their ideas, research, facts or story
- they feel daunted by the size of the project and the time they anticipate it will take to complete.

CREATING STRUCTURE

If you don't know how to structure your book or script, start by considering what more you need to learn and whether you have given your creative processes long enough to mull over your ideas. Are you rushing the creative process or do you really not know how to organize what you have? If a project needs more thinking time or more research then that's what it needs.

If you believe you have given enough time to research and to developing your ideas, consider how you can learn about the sort of structure you want or need to create. How you organize your project will depend on what the project is and what you want to achieve. How can you learn more about how to organize your particular ideas?

There is a multitude of books, courses and teachers that can offer guidance on both story structure and non-fiction writing. These can be very helpful, but don't stick slavishly to any formula unless you are targeting a market that demands something in a certain format. Courses, professional critiques and tutors can also be expensive and sometimes unhelpful, so research well if you decide to invest your money in seeking guidance. Also remember, you may be able to learn more from looking at what other people have already created and talking to other writers.

Insight

If you're working on a book or script, you don't have to understand how everything in it works or goes together before you start.

ADDRESSING FEELINGS OF BEING OVERWHELMED

The following can help reduce the sense of intimidation you are feeling about the sheer size of your writing project:

1. Work through Chapters 6 and 7 to understand, address and remove the thoughts that are making the project feel so overwhelming.
2. Consider completing the project as a single goal and work your way through Chapter 5 starting at *Exercise 4 Write down your goals*. Use this and the exercises that follow it to identify steps to create your book or script that are small enough to feel comfortable and manageable. Focus on completing each step as you work on it, rather than thinking about what you have to do to complete the whole project.
3. Build strong motivation to keep you going over the weeks/ months ahead using some of the ideas from the section *Twenty ways to boost your motivation* in Chapter 8.

Coaching experience

Ella wanted to write a novel around a busy family life and a part-time job as a librarian. She knew that it would take a long time to complete and believed it would use all of her free time. She considered she would never have any time to relax and pursue interests that didn't involve the children. Ella questioned whether it was worth starting at all and said that if she did, it would be 'a long hard slog' and was unsure she could keep going.

(Contd)

Ella initially considered her goals and values to ensure that she really wanted to write the novel. She then considered her thoughts that told her it wasn't worth starting, that it would be a long hard slog and that she wouldn't be able to keep going. As she reflected, she realized that she didn't have a time limit for completing her novel and that she didn't have to use all her free time to write.

Acknowledging that she had two choices, to give up on writing the novel (at least for now) or start writing, Ella set herself a routine of writing 1000 words each weekday evening immediately after the children had gone to bed. She gave herself two weekday evenings off a month to see friends and every weekend evening. She also planned to ensure at least one weekend evening was special in some way, so she and her partner really appreciated the break.

To address the feeling that this would be a long hard slog, Ella created and visualized a metaphor of her jogging up the stairs in a tall building. She didn't know how tall the building was, but the top disappeared in white fluffy clouds, which she considered magical and filled with her dreams of being a novelist. She used the metaphor as a daily visualization, seeing herself jogging effortlessly up the stairs, going higher and higher each day.

Inevitably, the ups and downs of family life prevented Ella writing as often as she planned. But she stuck to her routine whenever possible and, in just over seven months, she completed her first draft.

Note

Before you embark on any large writing project, ensure that it is aligned with your long-term goals. Even if it is, also check how it impacts on your other priorities and make sure there isn't a better option to achieve the results you are aiming for.

Making decisions

Decision making can be extremely complex, and sometimes there is no 'right' answer. So approach the following exercises as a detective, picking out what helps, discarding what doesn't, and find the best clarity you can before taking the plunge. As you work through the exercises, write your thoughts in your contemplation journal to help you gain better clarity.

VALUES AND DECISIONS

Knowing your core values can help you understand why projects appeal to you on a personal level. If you've done the work in Chapter 3 and identified your values, Exercise 1 which follows may be of help in your decision-making process. However, knowing your values isn't essential to completing the work in this chapter, it's just one way of helping you to assess your priorities. If you haven't identified your core values, you can still use the rest of the decision-making exercises in this chapter. If this is the case, move on to *Thinking patterns* which follows Exercise 1.

EXERCISE 1: PERSONAL VALUES

Identify which of your core values are aligned with each project under consideration. Does knowing which values are satisfied by each project suggest an obvious priority between the projects?

Insight

Because our personal values provide us with the motivation to achieve our goals, comparing our choices with our values can help identify which will be a more enjoyable project and, ultimately, a more satisfying achievement.

THINKING PATTERNS

People make choices all the time and barely even notice they're making them: what to wear, what to have for breakfast, whether to have chips or salad. At the other extreme, decisions can rattle round in our heads like an unravelled ball of wool becoming more and more tangled each time we attempt to gain focus. When this happens we need to sit down and untangle our bundle of thoughts, knot by knot.

Coaching experience

Scriptwriter Li was torn between developing two film ideas. He compared how each project satisfied his values. Despite identifying that one idea aligned far more strongly with his core values, Li still felt a powerful pull towards working on the other idea. Further reflection led him to identify that this idea was

(Contd)

potentially more lucrative. But Li was not strongly attached to the financial outcome. He reflected even further, considering the reasons he might think the money was important.

Li knew that his parents were concerned that he would never make a decent living from writing. This led him to realize that his desire to work on the more profitable idea was motivated by his desire to please them. This clarity allowed Li to recognize that in order to satisfy his true ambitions, he needed to go with the less commercial project. He also chose to explain his motivation to his parents in order to help allay their worries about him.

EXERCISE 2: EXPLORE YOUR THINKING

Consider each of the four lists of questions that follow for one of the projects you are deciding between. When you have worked to the end of all four lists for one project, answer the same questions for the next project. Work in this way until you have reflected on all the projects you want to decide between.

Once you have answered all the questions for all the projects under consideration, you will be guided to draw your thoughts together. However, do reflect on your answers as you find them. Don't just wait for the end. You may find clarity before this. And even if you don't, ongoing reflection is necessary to make the process as useful as possible.

LIST 1: GUT REACTIONS

Note your immediate reaction to each of the following questions:

- How would it feel to complete this project?
- Score on a scale of 1 to 10 how much you want to complete this project. (10 = I have to complete it, 1 = I really don't care if I complete it or not.)
- If you won the lottery tomorrow, would you still want to complete this project?
- If your answer to the lottery question was 'no', what would you do instead? Does this tell you there is something else you'd rather be spending your time on – writing project or otherwise?

LIST 2: PROS AND CONS

Using a fresh side of A4 for each project, write a list of the reasons to work on it and a list of reasons not to.

Anything else to add?

LIST 3: WHAT DO YOU WANT?

The following questions may appear to ask the same question twice, but there is a difference between 'want' and 'should'. 'Should' is what you think is the right thing to do. 'Want' is what you want to do irrespective of repercussions. For each project under consideration, ask yourself:

- What are the reasons I *should* do it?
- What are the reasons I *shouldn't* do it?
- What are the reasons I *want* to do it?
- What are the reasons I *don't want* to do it?
- What do others expect of me?
- How does completing this project serve me in the long term?
- Where will completing this project lead me to?
- How does not completing this project serve me in the long term?
- Where will not completing this project lead me to?
- Will this project take me closer to achieving my long-term goals?
- Give an immediate yes/no response to the question, 'Is this something I really want to do?'

LIST 4: HOW DOES IT FEEL?

Ask, for each project:

- What scares me about working on or completing this project?
- What excites me about working on or completing this project?
- Am I drawn to this project because it is the safest option?

CALL YOUR OWN BLUFF

If you only have two projects under consideration, after you've answered the earlier lists of questions for both projects, flip a coin. If it lands heads up you make one choice, tails up you take the other. Pay close attention to how you feel when the coin lands. What do you say to yourself? Are you pleased or do you think you should flip again and go for the best of three?

CONCLUSIONS

Once you have worked through the questions above for each project under consideration, use the following questions to help you reflect on the answers you have given.

- Which project is most strongly aligned with your core values? (You can only answer this question if you have done the work in Chapter 3. Ignore this question if you haven't.)

- Which project would be best for your long-term future?
- Which project scares you most?*
- Which project excites you most?
- Score again on a scale of 1 to 10 your gut feeling of how much you want to complete each project or achieve its outcome. (Has this changed from when you scored it in List 1?)
- Which project do you want to give priority to?
- Which project are you going to give priority to?

*If you recognize that you are not doing something that you need or want to do, because it scares you or takes you out of your comfort zone, look at the section *What's stopping you?* in Chapter 6. Considering each fear you have as something that's 'stopping you', work through from here to the end of Chapter 7.

HAVE YOU MADE A DECISION?

Can you now decide which project to work on? If you have decided, congratulate yourself on making a decision and get going.

If you still haven't come to a firm conclusion, the work you have done will have stirred up your thinking and prompted your subconscious to work in new directions. This should at least help you become a little clearer, and possibly prompt a moment of insight in the near future as you continue to consider your decision. You can also consider whether you are holding back because of the following:

There is something you don't want to do
If this is the case, go to the section *What's stopping you?* in Chapter 6. Consider what you don't want to do as what is 'stopping you' and work through from here to the end of Chapter 7.

You doubt your decision-making abilities
If you have a tendency to think you can't make decisions or think you don't make good decisions, take a look at the Chapter 7. This will show you how to deal with the thinking that holds you back from decision making.

You need to learn or know something more
Ask yourself, 'What do I need to do or to know to make this decision?' If you come up with an answer, repeat the question until you can find no more answers and take appropriate action on whatever answer(s) you come up with.

IF YOU STILL HAVEN'T MADE A DECISION

Remember, even not making a decision is a choice. You may have good reason not to decide for now. However, continuing to sit on the fence once you have reflected from all angles is almost always a choice not to progress with your writing. Ensure you are not using indecision as a method of procrastination.

If the words still don't flow

If you are still 'stuck' after working with the relevant parts of this chapter, or you feel you can't find a relevant part, consider whether you have a hidden fear that is stopping you. Ask yourself:

- What do I fear about working on this?
- What do I fear will happen if this piece of work fails?
- What do I fear will happen if I succeed with this piece of work?

If any of these questions lead you to identify something you fear, ask the question repeatedly until you come up with no more new answers.

If you find that you have any fear(s) that are holding you back, turn to the section *What's stopping you?* in Chapter 6. Considering each fear you have as something that's 'stopping you', work through from here to the end of Chapter 7.

10 THINGS TO REMEMBER

1. Being 'blocked' or 'stuck' means different things to different people.
2. Keeping your motivation and creativity high can prevent you from getting stuck in the first place.
3. The more you think or talk about yourself being stuck or blocked the more likely you are to stay that way.
4. Sometimes asking a question of your subconscious and not thinking about your challenge is all you need do to free your thinking.
5. Having previously written a successful book or script can cause as many concerns about writing the next one as having previously written an unsuccessful one.
6. Before you embark on any large writing project, ensure that it is aligned with your long-term goals.
7. If a project feels too large or overwhelming, ask yourself, 'What more do I need to learn about the story/my ideas?' and 'What more do I need to learn about creating structure?'
8. If you're working on a large project, you don't have to understand how everything in it works or goes together before you start.
9. Not making a decision can be a way of procrastinating.
10. Fears about working on a piece of writing, or it succeeding or failing, may be at the root of your inability to move forward.

13

Dealing more effectively with rejection

In this chapter you will learn:

- ***why rejection can have a detrimental influence on us and on our writing***
- ***to understand factors that influence your reaction to rejection***
- ***how to handle rejection more effectively.***

All writers and aspiring writers know rejection is part of the deal. We experience it repeatedly from first submission all the way to publishing a book that doesn't sell or writing a film or play that fails. Wherever we are in our writing journey, whatever our previous achievements, rejection still has the potential to strike and the power to hurt, demotivate and reduce self-esteem.

> ***Writers do two major things – write and get rejected. That's how it works. I mean, if you choose this, especially as a career, you can virtually write it on the to-do list. Write article, open the post, get rejections. So what I've always found annoying is that some – not all, some – really do still upset me.***
>
> Gill Smith

Have you ever held back on your feelings over rejection? Have you ever told yourself, 'I shouldn't be behaving/thinking/feeling like this'? Have you ever suppressed emotion over being turned down? And if you have got angry, or cried, or vented in some other way, did you then feel embarrassed or get mad with yourself for doing it?

Maybe you've said things like, 'I shouldn't be angry', 'I should be in control', 'I ought to be getting on with my life', 'Other writers don't behave like this.'

The trouble with 'shoulds' and 'oughts' is they're exactly that; they're what we think we 'should' or 'ought to' do, not what we want to do. But why 'should' we? We get hurt and angry for a reason and we need to acknowledge it.

Insight

It's not just obvious rejections, such as work being turned down, that can throw us off kilter. Negative feedback, such as bad reviews, or modifications by people like editors or directors, all tell us our work isn't good enough and can elicit a rejection reaction.

Universal reasons rejection hurts

IT'S PERSONAL

Rejection tells us someone doesn't like something about what we've written or our writing doesn't come up to the expected standard. Either way we feel judged; someone or something says we're not good enough. That makes it very personal, and when personal stuff happens we tend to get emotional.

WE'VE FAILED

Rejection means we haven't achieved what we set out to achieve. We might be able to approach someone else or create a more successful piece in the future, but in the short term someone pushed us a step further away from our goals. That's bound to smart.

IT TAKES US OUT OF THE GAME

Any time we're rejected it takes us away from a part of the world we were involved with or we wanted to become involved in. As human beings we have a psychological need to be connected to the world around us. When we see these connections being broken, or we fail to forge them, we experience stress as we are no longer a player in that game.

The bottom line always comes back to us, however right or wrong we believe the person or circumstance that rejects our writing, however much we care about the piece. Rejection sends us a negative message about ourselves.

Rejection really does hurt

Researchers at the University of California ran an experiment where volunteers were asked to play a computer game where they caught and threw a ball with two other players. The participants thought they were interacting with other volunteers. In reality, the other two players were controlled by a computer.

The volunteers were told they could throw the ball to the player of their choosing, but after they had received the ball seven times, the computer stopped throwing the ball to them.

As they played, the volunteers' brains were scanned to detect changes in blood flow to various parts of the brain. After the computerized rejection, the scan detected increased activity in two areas of the brain linked to physical pain.

The results of this experiment don't mean our brain registers rejection exactly the same way as physical pain. But it does show that even a trivial instance of rejection provokes a reaction linked to the same alarm system that is set off when we experience physical pain.

Personal reasons rejection hurts

PAST EXPERIENCE

In one way and another we all experience rejection in our personal lives. We can experience rejection from our peers, employer, a parent, a sibling, a partner – the list is endless. Even though having our writing rejected is unlikely to be related to these rejections, it can still stir up memories of them on an emotional level. However, because the recognition is on an emotional level, we register the emotion, but not always the reason.

If you recognize that you are still coming to terms with rejection in another area of your life, be aware that this is likely to impact on the emotions you feel when you receive a writing rejection.

ATTACHMENT TO RESULTS

If we didn't care that we were rejected, then we wouldn't have chased the project in the first place. On top of this, the more attached we are to the result, or the more important it is to achieve a result with a certain piece of writing, the more emotional our reaction to rejection is likely to be.

ATTACHMENT TO YOUR WRITING

Our writing is important to us; it's something born of us, something we have created. Sometimes it's just a job of work, but sometimes we care much more deeply. If someone rejects a writing project that we are strongly attached to, we can feel a bit like a mother feels when her child gets passed over for a lead role in the school play. It's not you being rejected, but it still feels like it.

THE PLACE YOU ARE AT RIGHT NOW

If the rest of our life is dumping on us, a rejection letter is just one more piece of proof that life is bad, we'll never achieve, no one appreciates us, recognizes our talent, etc, etc, etc.

YOUR LEVEL OF SELF-ESTEEM

Self-esteem is rather like amour which life takes shots at. Rejection of our writing is one of those bullets. Creating or maintaining high levels of self-esteem will help keep rejection feeling more like you've been hit by a spud gun than an armour-piercing rifle.

VALUES

Rejection can also impact on our core values, because our values have a strong influence over our emotions. If rejection confronts one or more of them it is likely to elicit a negative emotional response.

If you've worked on identifying your core values in Chapter 3, consider how the general experience of rejection will impact on them. Knowing this should help you understand your emotional reaction to rejection more clearly in the future. It may also be worth considering if you have any values that link to a specific piece of work, if its rejection causes a particularly strong reaction.

Real life

Believing that she had failed every time she received a rejection made Trisha feel her value of achievement was being discredited.

Sami hated receiving standard informal rejections to all his hard work. This confronted his values of originality and respect. Sami's value of respect was further confronted when he was dropped, but not informed, by a syndicate who sold his work.

Jo was unable to fulfil her values of sharing and communication when her work was rejected.

Just knowing how our values are confronted by rejection can reduce the emotion we experience in future. However, next time you are rejected, look back at your values and consider how that rejection has specifically interacted with them.

Creating a strong rejection strategy

STEP 1: REDUCE THE LIKELIHOOD OF REJECTION

Before you start writing, always ensure that you have fully researched the market you're aiming for.

As you write, keep your chosen market in mind and, if you're targeting a specific publication, ensure that you tailor the work as perfectly as you can for it. Never make it more generic, because you know there are other publications you can send it to if your first choice rejects it. However, as you do your initial research, make a list of who else you could approach. This will save time later if your first choice rejects your work.

> ***Initially I targeted 100 Ways For A Dog To Train Its Human at publishers of small gift books. I sent it to four publishers before realizing that my approach was wrong (none of those publishers printed books about animals). I found a potential publisher and rewrote my manuscript again (this was the fifth time) to ensure that it matched the style of my target publisher. They took it.***
>
> Simon Whaley

Once you believe your work is ready to submit, imagine you're critiquing it for another writer and consider:

- Does the title entice me to read this?
- Am I hooked from the first line?
- What pulls me into the piece?
- Where do I switch off?
- How can this piece be improved?
- What could be better about my pitch?

Make any necessary changes and submit your work only when you believe it really is the best it can be.

Once you've submitted a piece of writing or a proposal, forget about it and start something new.

Insight

Remember, there are an enormous number of unsolicited manuscripts received by producers, editors and agents every year. If you are submitting speculatively it is essential that your submission meets the criteria of what they're looking for and it must truly stand out to get noticed.

STEP 2: WHEN YOU GET REJECTED

Sit quietly and acknowledge any feelings you have about the rejection. Don't tell yourself you need to be tough and ignore them, but equally don't overplay them or take them out on yourself or anyone else. Also consider if any of the reasons named in the section *Personal reasons rejection hurts*, above, are influencing this particular rejection. You may find it helps to use your contemplation journal to write about how you feel in order to bring yourself to a better understanding.

Rejection can cause you to act irrationally

Researchers at Case Western Reserve University in Ohio have found that rejection can lower IQ scores and increase aggression.

In the first experiment a group of strangers were allowed to get to know each other, then separated. Each person was asked to list the two other people in the group they would like to work with. They were then either told that everyone had chosen to work with them or no one had chosen to work with them.

In a second experiment, participants were given a personality test and were told that the results showed they would end up alone in life or surrounded by friends and family.

In both experiments, the aggression scores of the rejected participants increased, their IQ scores dropped by approximately 25 per cent and their analytical reasoning scores dropped by 30 per cent.

Dispelling emotion

Once you've considered your feelings, you may find the following exercise helpful in assisting you to dispel any negativity.

Sit quietly and jot down in your contemplation journal how you feel. Don't write a long piece, just use single words such as infuriated, frustrated, blue, lonely, heartbroken, smothered, cheated ... use whatever word(s) seem right for you (don't use these examples unless they really fit what you are experiencing).

Once you've named how you feel, close your eyes and scan your body with your mind. Where is the emotion you have named? Stomach? Ribs? Throat? Chest? Somewhere else? Make a mental note of exactly where you find the feeling and what it feels like. For example, it may be like a cold stone, a burning anger or a constriction. Once again, make sure you use the words that ring true for you.

Using a scale of 1 to 10, score how strongly you are experiencing the emotion(s) you have named. (10 = couldn't feel it more strongly, 1 = I don't feel it at all.)

Keeping your eyes closed, focus on the feeling and imagine it fading from you. If it feels hot, imagine it growing colder; if it feels cold, imagine it growing warmer; if it is moving then let it grow calm. Imagine the feeling flowing out of you into the room then away out of the building.

STEP 3: LEARN FROM REJECTION

Wait until you're feeling level headed again before you reflect on what you can learn from your rejection.

If you receive feedback

Publishers, agents, editors and other people we send our work to are all busy people. If you submit speculatively, they rarely have time for personal replies when they reject your work. If you do receive some feedback in these circumstances, take it as a good sign that they took time out of their busy schedule to encourage you and that you're heading in the right direction.

Whatever circumstances you receive feedback under, ask:

- What did they like about the piece?
- What didn't they like?
- How can I use this feedback to improve the piece before I send it out again?
- How does this feedback apply to my writing in general?

Insight

When our work is returned to us, we have often moved on. Receiving a rejection can give us fresh perspective on our submission. Taking time to review what we submitted and how we submitted it can give us useful information and ideas to act on in the future.

Whether you receive personal feedback or not, look again at the piece you submitted. Imagine again you're critiquing it for another writer. Reconsider:

- Does the title entice me to read this?
- Am I hooked from the first line?
- What pulls me into the piece?
- Where do I switch off?
- What could be better about my pitch?

Also ask:

- In hindsight, was the person I approached the best person to approach?
- What do I need to change and/or improve, before I resubmit elsewhere?
- What steps can I take to improve my writing and/or pitching in general?

Once you've decided on what changes you need to make, take action and resubmit elsewhere (or send back to the person that returned it, if they invited you to). Keep writing, keep putting out more work and using what you learn to make every submission better than the last one.

Note

Remember also that rejection often comes down to personal tastes or current requirements rather than flaws in your submission.

> ***I sold an article to the very same editor, at the very same magazine, who'd rejected it ten years previously. I hadn't changed my text at all. What I've learned is that 'no' means 'not for me at this particular moment in time'. It does not mean 'never'.***
>
> Simon Whaley

10 THINGS TO REMEMBER

1. As writers we experience rejection at many stages of the process of getting our work published or performed.
2. Rejection affects us for both personal and universal reasons.
3. The first step to building a strong rejection strategy is to reduce your chances of rejection when you create a piece of writing.
4. Once you've submitted a piece, forget about it and start something new.
5. If you're submitting speculatively, it is essential that your submission meets the submission criteria and it must really stand out to get noticed.
6. Don't deny feelings associated with rejection if you have them, but don't overplay them or overreact either.
7. Some rejections may affect you differently from others.
8. Wait until you're feeling level headed before reflecting on what you can learn from a rejection.
9. Receiving personal feedback is a good sign that someone took the time from a busy schedule to encourage you and to help you improve.
10. If you want to be successful you need to keep writing, keep putting out more work and using what you learn to make every submission better than the last.

14

Letting go

In this chapter you will learn:
- *why you could be procrastinating even though you are writing*
- *how to understand your process more fully*
- *to reduce the tendency to keep changing elements of a piece*
- *to build better focus on a single project.*

Writing, like most things in life, usually takes longer than you think, but sometimes we ourselves can make this process take even more time by:

- constantly making minor changes, because we think a piece isn't good enough or isn't ready
- getting stuck on the same piece, because we are continually changing the plot, characters, structure etc
- moving on to new pieces of writing before we've finished the previous one(s)
- holding back from submitting.

Could you be writing yet still procrastinating?

Take out your contemplation journal and ask yourself the following questions:

- What are the advantages of not finishing a piece of writing?
- What do I fear about finishing?
- What do I fear about my writing being successful?
- Am I avoiding submitting or producing finished pieces?

If you recognize from your answers that you avoid completing writing projects or hold back from submitting, start at the section *What are you thinking?* in Chapter 6 and work on to the end of Chapter 7. This will enable you to explore and address your concerns. However, when you take the steps outlined in the section *What are you thinking?* don't consider all your thoughts about your writing challenges. Just consider the reasons you avoid completing writing projects or why you hold back from submitting, whichever is appropriate.

If you haven't found any evidence that you're procrastinating, consider the relevant section(s) which follow.

If you're constantly making minor changes

Coaching experience

Jenny came to coaching because she had over 60 short stories on her computer. She knew they were all but ready to send out, but she never submitted them, because she always wanted to give them one more edit. She chose to tackle the situation by getting one story up to standard within a week and sending it out.

When Jenny looked at the story she had chosen to work on, she found the last three rewrites had created three versions with almost no differences between them. She also realized this wasn't the only story she had written with more than one almost-identical twin. Jenny recognized she was wasting a colossal amount of time as well as never getting any of her stories out.

Letting your writing go can be tough. It's quite normal to feel apprehensive before you finally send a piece off. This is hardly surprising. Competition is high in all fields of writing and producing what is wanted is an imprecise science. We therefore need to submit the best work we possibly can. Nevertheless, it's important to recognize when the drive for excellence tips over into extreme perfectionism.

> ***In a survey of 56 writers, 18 (32 per cent) said they put off submitting.***
>
> The Write Coach

As writers we can't afford to put out shoddy, ill-informed pieces of work. We need to scrutinize our writing for errors and ill-formed prose. We also need to strive for excellence, and getting facts right is crucial. But does our writing need to be perfect? Does perfect exist? And if it does, is your perfect the same as another writer's perfect?

If you recognize or suspect you rewrite beyond a sensible point, work through the following exercise.

STEP 1

Before you start your next new piece of writing, note down in your contemplation journal the answers to the following:

- What do I want to achieve with this piece of writing?
- Who is my audience?
- Is there a message or some awareness I want this piece to raise? If so, what is it?
- What are my reasons for writing this?

STEP 2

When you finish the first draft, note in your contemplation journal what you have just achieved in the broadest terms. For example, created a structure, dumped the story out of your head, organized your research, explored your ideas more fully…

STEP 3

When you finish the second draft, again note what you have achieved. For example, you may now have made the piece more coherent or rearranged it into a better order.

STEP 4

For every subsequent draft ask, 'What have I achieved by redrafting this?' As you move through this process, consider:

- when the piece achieves its goals
- when it reaches 'almost ready to part with'
- how much longer you continue to work on it once it is 'almost ready to part with'
- when you start to over-rewrite
- the reasons you start to over-rewrite.

Completing this exercise can help you:

- learn more about your process
- recognize when you begin to work on a piece of writing longer than is necessary
- recognize something you are unsure of about relating to your writing – if you do, take action to address these concerns.

Note

You may wish to repeat the exercise over several pieces of work to learn more about your personal creative process.

Insight

There is no 'right' number of drafts for any piece of writing. The way to give yourself the greatest chance of success is to focus on becoming the best writer you can be and making your work as good as you can get it before you send it out.

If you're constantly making major changes

Coaching experience

Screenwriter turned aspiring novelist Hari had received great feedback on his early work from some impressive people. However, he was failing to develop it further. He said:

'I have repeatedly come up with strong ideas for novels (according to what others say), and I manage to bring them to a rough first draft. But when it comes to really isolating the central theme of the story, I block.

'I rewrite the same story a thousand times, using the same characters but differently every time. I change the set up, I change from comedy to drama, I switch the main character to a minor, but nothing ever works. Instead of advancing, this gruesome process usually brings me very deep frustration and despair, because I am capable of rewriting the first chapter every day of the week, and every week of the year!'

FINDING DEEPER UNDERSTANDING

If you recognize that you are constantly making big changes to a writing project, the following exercise can help build focus. However, also consider that this is an area where learning more about creating work in your chosen area may be more appropriate.

Using your contemplation journal, ask yourself:

- What are the fundamental things I write about?
- If I were a 'brand of writer' what brand would I write?
- What are the common theme(s) throughout my writing?

- What do I want others to gain from having encountered my writing?
- Am I constantly chasing trends or what I think other people want?

Ask of the project you're currently working on:

- What are the specific messages?
- What are the story arcs?
- Whose story is this?
- How do the threads of the story tie into the final chapter/paragraph/scene?

Also look back and identify the scenes/chapters/events/ideas you need to draw out to build good rhythm and pace through the piece.

Note
Knowing your values may be useful in helping you clarify some of your answers to the questions above. Chapter 3 will show you how to identify your values if you have not done so already.

Reflect on your answers to the earlier questions to see if they help you identify what you want to write or how you want to write the piece under consideration. If they do, create a short description or make notes about what you need to do with the piece. For example, include whose point of view you are going to tell a story from, or what storylines you want to add or remove, or the style of the piece.

Insight

Taking time at the outset to consider what you are writing, why you are writing it and to experiment with the way you are writing the piece, can make it easier to write it in the long run.

If you're constantly moving to new writing before anything is truly finished

> ***It's so easy to move beyond the present when things start getting difficult and say, 'Actually, that other story is more likely to be commercial. I should be working on that one.' Thus, none of them get finished.***
>
> Benjamin Scott

Do you move from working on one idea to another, never, or very rarely, progressing anything to a stage where it's ready to submit?

The best way to ensure that you break this habit is to set goals. Because if you don't know where you're going, you are likely to be constantly pulled in the direction which is currently most attractive and, as the idea you're working on grows older, new ideas will become more appealing.

Chapters 1 to 5 of this book show you how to set both long- and short-term goals for your writing ambitions to help you stay focused. Using Chapter 8 to build long-term motivation will also help you stay focused on the writing project in hand.

Alongside setting goals and building long-term motivation, it can also help to ask the following questions at the start of a new project, noting your answers in your contemplation journal for future reference:

- What do I want to achieve here?
- What are the reasons this is important to me?
- What are the reasons this is important to others?
- How does this contribute to my longer-term goals?
- How does it fulfil my values?

If, later on, you find yourself tempted to put the project to one side before it's finished, or send it out when it's not up to scratch, reflect on your answers to these questions to help motivate you to stay with it. Also ask yourself, 'How will I achieve my goals if I never bring anything up to a high enough standard?'

Note

You shouldn't feel you have to stick slavishly to any one piece of writing. Sometimes we do need to discard or leave certain work to one side. This can be:

- when it needs a rest, so we can come back to it afresh
- when we see a truly better opportunity to achieve our goals
- when a piece really isn't working
- when the market for that work disappears.

If you realize that you genuinely need to leave a piece of writing and move on, do so, but consider the same questions before you start your next project.

FINAL WORD

If you have projects you keep going back to and progressing a little, but never get them finished, take a look at 'Get rid of mental clutter', in the section *Twenty ways to boost your motivation*, in Chapter 8.

10 THINGS TO REMEMBER

1 Even if you are continually working on your writing it can still be a form of procrastination.

2 It's normal to feel apprehensive when you part with your work.

3 Observing and analyzing your progress can help you stop over-rewriting.

4 Failing to part with your work can be a sign that you need to address fears about success and/or failure and/or concerns about your abilities as a writer.

5 Always submit work of the highest standard you can achieve.

6 There is no 'right' number of drafts for any piece of writing.

7 Identifying your motivation for working on a writing project at the outset can help maintain focus as you write.

8 It's fine to move on to new projects if you are genuinely allowing yourself a break and if you do go back to finish the previous project in a reasonable timeframe.

9 If you have a tendency to abandon work before it's finished, maintaining awareness of the bigger goals it links to can help you stay focused.

10 Analyzing your thoughts can help you deal with a tendency to keep writing but rarely/never submitting.

15

Creating a personal plan

In this chapter you will learn:
- ***to embed the changes you want to make in your life.***

Any of the work you do in this book, or any of the suggestions you take on, will enable you to make changes about yourself and your writing habits. Sometimes changes are easy to make, sometimes they can take a while to implement, sometimes we think we've made them but then return to our old ways. Making a personal plan is a good way to ensure that you create enduring transformation in your life.

Making your plan

STEP 1: WHAT HAVE YOU LEARNED?

Reflect on what you have learned from this book. This could run from having worked all the way through and lost count of how much you have learned, to just deciding to take on board one idea.

STEP 2: YOUR TOP TEN LEARNINGS

Use your contemplation journal to make a list of up to ten learnings you have gained from *Coach Yourself to Writing Success*.

Note

A learning is a single change that you want, or have started, to bring into your life. For example, you may consider, having worked through Chapters 1 to 5, that how to use goal setting is one learning. Alternatively, one learning could come from reading a single page or less, such as learning to make appointments with yourself.

STEP 3: YOUR MOST IMPORTANT CHANGE

Once you have created your list, identify the order of importance you give to making the changes on your list.

Check that you are fully familiar with what you need to do to achieve the most important change you want to make. Also decide how you are going to remind yourself to work on it.

Depending on the adjustments you want to make, this one change may be all you realistically can pull into your life right now. However, if you can bring in more, do this in priority order, but keep in mind which single change is most important to achieve and give priority to working on it.

STEP 4: MAKE YOUR CHANGE(S)

Put a note in your diary each week to check if you have worked on the change(s) you have currently set your sights on.

Coaching tips

- ✓ One way to ensure that you bring the change(s) you desire into your life, is to make a list of 'rules' of what actions you need to take and place it somewhere you see it regularly. If the word 'rules' feels constricting, call this list whatever you like that inspires you.
- ✓ An alternative to having a list of 'rules', is to write each change you want to make as a precise, positive, personal, present tense sentence and place it where you will see it every day – if you want, you can add an action plan to remind yourself of the steps you need to take. This is effectively setting out your change as a goal. If you haven't done this already, use the rules explained in Exercise 4 in Chapter 5 to set your change as a goal and make an action plan to achieve it – see Exercise 6 in Chapter 5 for how to create an action plan.
- ✓ Depending on the change you are making, you may find it helpful to use Exercise 3 in Chapter 5 to reflect on any potential obstacles or challenges that you might encounter in making your change.

COACHING TIPS

Insight

I put a note of the goal(s) I need to focus on most strongly inside the door of my wardrobe. Each morning it reminds me what I need to do and keeps me on track.

STEP 5: REVIEW THE IMPACT OF YOUR ACTIONS

Once in a while, note the results you are achieving from the actions you are taking. (If you are working on goal setting, this will lead you to check the results at regular intervals anyway.) Congratulate yourself if the changes are working well. If they aren't having the influence you hoped, reflect on:

- whether you're taking sufficient action to implement the change
- how you could increase the effect your actions are having
- whether you need to make any additional change(s) to support your actions
- whether you need to make a completely different change.

If you discover that you aren't taking all the actions you planned to, and are working on more than one change, cut down the number you are working on. If you are working on just one change, ask yourself what you can do to ensure that in future you implement the habits and activities you want to take on board.

If you constantly fail to make changes, consider what's stopping you and how you can address it. If you truly struggle to implement a change, work through Chapter 6, but instead of considering your writing challenges in the section *What are you thinking?*, consider your challenge as not bringing the changes into your life that you want to make. If you find Chapter 6 useful, Chapter 7 can help reinforce any actions you choose to take.

STEP 6: MAKING FURTHER CHANGES

Once you have truly embedded a change in your life, look again at your top-ten list and decide on the next priority change to bring. Once you have completed making your top ten changes, consider what further changes you want to make and work in the same manner until you have embedded all the new learning you want to.

COACHING TIPS

Coaching tips

- ✓ If it takes a while to work through your top-ten list, you may discover that your priorities have altered when you return to it and you may need to assign different priorities, or even work on changes you haven't got on your list.

- ✓ Making changes always has a knock-on influence. Monitor the changes you make to ensure that they are having an all-round impact you are happy about.
- ✓ Sometimes the knock-on effect means that you return to your priority list and discover that by working on one change, you have brought about a change identified on your list that you weren't working on.

Future change

Life is never static; in the future you may well need and want to make further changes. Hopefully this book will be of use to you in that process. You may also find that modifications you make slip back out of your life. If they do, reflect on why you have let them go, then pull them back in, or make a new plan, depending on what your reflection reveals.

Insight

As a coach I believe it's important to walk my talk. But there are still times when I act against ways I know will nourish my writing and bring success. At these times, I remind myself I'm only human and make a plan to steer myself back on course.

10 THINGS TO REMEMBER

1. Taking on board too many changes at once can result in never bringing any of them into your life.
2. A learning is a single change you want to, or have started to, bring into your life.
3. It may only be realistic to pull one change into your life at a time.
4. Always maintain awareness of which single change is the most important to achieve.
5. Create a method of reminding yourself to take the actions you want to take.
6. Always ensure that the actions you take are having a positive impact on all aspects of your life.
7. If your actions aren't having the desired impact, reflect on what you need to do differently.
8. Your priorities may alter. Always ensure that the change(s) you are working on is/are a priority.
9. The adjustments you make may sometimes slip back out of your life. If they do, check the reasons for this then refocus and bring them back in, if appropriate.
10. If you find yourself moving away from your goals, refocus and steer yourself back in the right direction.

Appendix 1

Carrying out reviews

If you have set goals, it is essential to review them at least every three months to ensure that you are on track. You also need to identify new goals to aim for within the next three months. On top of this, it is important to perform an end-of-year review to focus fully on your progress, consider what you have learned and how you will take that learning forward into the future. If you want to, you can also carry out more regular reviews, weekly or monthly, whichever you prefer, and it can be helpful to do a little extra reflection at six-monthly intervals too.

Whatever reviewing you need or want to do, this appendix offers advice and insights to assist you. However, there are a few points it's important to bear in mind as you carry out any review:

1. Don't just stick to the questions suggested in this appendix. Use them as a framework to chart and consider the progress you are making, to discover different perspectives and find further questions to ask yourself.
2. Sometimes you won't have an answer to a question, because it doesn't apply for some reason.
3. It's imperative to take action as well as make plans.
4. The action you take doesn't need to be enormous. It's great if you take a giant stride, but no one can be taking giant strides all the time.
5. We rarely achieve what we set out to accomplish in exactly the manner we thought we would.
6. We constantly need to reassess what we've achieved, where we are heading and what we want.
7. If you haven't got the results you were hoping for, there's always something to learn from your experience. When things don't go your way, ask, 'What have I learned?' and 'How can that leaning help me move forward?' Don't dwell on the past. Reflect on the learning experience and move on.
8. If you find you are steering yourself away from your goals, reassess what you want to accomplish. Identify how you can

steer yourself back on course or what new routes you want to take, if you realize your goals have changed.

WEEKLY/MONTHLY REVIEWS

If you enjoy keeping track of your progress, the following review can be used either weekly or monthly.

Use your contemplation journal to reflect on the following questions:

- What did I achieve this week/month?
- Do I need to make any adjustments to my goals or action plans going forward?
- What do I want to achieve over the next week/month?
- What steps will I take during the next week/month?

THREE-MONTHLY REVIEWS

Use your contemplation journal to reflect on the following questions:

- What have I achieved over the last three months?
- What progress have I made with my writing during the last three months?
- What have I learned from the last three months' progress and/or achievements?
- What else have I learned regarding my writing?
- What will I do differently in future, because of this learning?
- What goals do I want/need to achieve over the next three months?

Return to the notes you made when working on Exercise 5 in Chapter 5. Identify the goals you need to achieve in the next three months. Ensure that they are written as personal, precise, present tense, positive statements and create an action plan for each as explained in Exercise 6, Chapter 5. However, if you are 'experimenting' either:

- continue to experiment
- create new goals
- adjust your goals as appropriate.

Check your commitment to your goals

Score on a scale of 1 to 10 how committed you are to each of the writing, or writing-related, actions you are currently working on, or planning to work on, in the next three months. (10 = absolutely sure I'm going to do this, 1 = I know I'm not going to do it.)

If your score is 10, you're fully committed.

If you score 7–9, ask yourself, 'What can I do to increase my commitment to this action?' It's fine if you can't raise your score; you're still likely to complete the action. However, making your motivation as strong as possible should make your goals easier to accomplish and give you a stronger chance of completing them, if something does knock your motivation.

If you score 6 or below, ask yourself, 'What can I do to increase my commitment to this action?' Once you have found a way to increase your commitment, rescore it. If it is still less than 7, ask yourself, 'Do I really want to take this action?'

ANSWER 'YES'

Use your contemplation journal to explore the reasons your commitment is so low and how you can raise it.

Add any action(s) you have decided to take to increase your commitment to your plans to achieve the goal(s) they relate to.

Note

If your commitment score remains below 7, you're unlikely to find the motivation to complete the action in question.

ANSWER 'NO'

Review what you truly want to achieve by going back to the start of Part one. If necessary, work on any exercises you find relevant or helpful.

If goal setting is too rigid for you

If you have chosen not to set short-term goals, review the progress you have made over the last three months. Ask yourself these additional questions:

- Is my progress satisfactory?
- Am I keeping up with the deadlines I have set?
- Do I need to change the deadlines I have set?
- Am I being honest with myself, or is not setting goals an excuse not to work on my writing?

Values

Use your contemplation journal to ask yourself, 'How does the writing I am working on right now fulfil my values?' If you're not happy with the answer, consider how you could make your values connect more strongly to it, or if you need to review your priorities.

SIX-MONTH REVIEW

As well as carrying out the activities suggested for three-monthly reviews, it's also useful to look back six months after you first start setting goals or six months after you set your yearly goals and consider these additional questions:

- Am I on target to complete this year's goals on time?
- Are there any deadlines I can realistically assign an earlier date to?
- Are there any deadlines I need to move back?
- Are there any goals I want to add to what I will achieve this year?
- Are there any goals I need to remove or modify?

YEARLY REVIEW

Note in your contemplation journal what you have achieved regarding your writing for each month of the last year. This includes action you have taken as well as actual writing 'successes'.

Take a look at what you have achieved, congratulate yourself on your progress, then use your creativity journal to reflect on the following questions about the year that has just gone by:

- What steps did I take to get closer to my writing ambitions?
- How has my writing grown?
- How have I grown as a writer?
- What have been the highs and lows relating to my writing?
- What obstacles did I overcome, both personal and related to my writing?
- What have I learned about my writing?
- What have I learned about myself as a person?
- What did I learn about writing from others?

For anything that makes you feel you 'failed', ask the following extra questions:

- What didn't work out as I planned/hoped?
- What are the reasons it didn't work?
- What could I have done differently so I did get the result I was looking for?
- What have I learned/gained from this experience?
- How will I take this learning forward into the future?

- What do I want to do now? Find or implement a new approach, or make adjustments to what I'm aiming for?
- What will be the consequences of this decision?

Support

Review the support you have had over the last year by reflecting on the following sets of questions:

- When do I allow circumstances or others to slow me down or distract me from my goals?
- What can I do to prevent these influences having the same impact next year?
- What do I do to sabotage my goals?
- What can I do to stop my self-sabotage?
- Who are my supporters?
- Do I show my appreciation to my supporters?
- Do I need to find more support for my writing? If so, how am I going to do it?

Moving forward

Once you have fully reflected on last year's progress and what you have learned from it, ask yourself the following:

- How can I capitalize on what I learned/gained over the last year?
- What will I do differently in future?

Goals and action plans

Look back to the outline for success you created in Chapter 1 and the overview of your future goals created in Chapter 5 Exercise 2. Use your contemplation journal to consider:

- Have I changed my mind about anything I want to achieve?
- Do I want to add, change or take anything away from my future plans?
- Can I foresee any obstacles to achieving my goals, because I have modified them or because I know or recognize something that I did not know last year? If so, identify what actions you need to take to overcome them and add these actions to your plans. If the obstacles seem truly insurmountable, use Exercise 3 in Chapter 5 to address this.

Now return to Chapter 5 and repeat Exercises 5 and 6.

Appendix 2

Positive language

Chapter 6 identifies some of the language that is commonly related to limiting thinking. Along with Chapter 7, it shows you how to identify and address the messages these words and phrases are giving. However, it is not just the language identified in Chapter 6 that reveals underlying limiting thinking. The following list provides a more comprehensive overview of language to listen out for and eliminate once you've become familiar with techniques explained in Chapters 6 and 7. It also gives a quick reference guide on how to challenge what you hear and can be used to check that you're using entirely positive language when you set goals. This appendix can also be used if you were unable to identify the root of a negative thought when you analyzed your thinking in Chapter 6.

NOTES/REMINDERS

- There will always be instances when a word that can reveal negativity is being used in a positive context and does not need attention. The challenges suggested below should help you recognize if this is the case. But either way, if you make the language you use sound more positive, it will have a more positive impact on your confidence and self-esteem and on the message you give about yourself to others.
- You may need to look back at Chapter 6 to find a deeper personal explanation of the thinking behind some of the words or phrases which follow. If you do, see 'Analyze your thinking' in the section *What are you thinking?*
- Looking back at Chapter 6 will also remind you how to take action to make changes to overcome any fears or obstacles you discover. See the sections *What's stopping you?* and *Taking action against thoughts that limit success.*
- Chapter 7 discusses how to remove and replace the thoughts/ language you have identified.

Limiting language

CAN'T/UNABLE

Saying 'I can't' or 'I'm unable' immediately stops us thinking that we might be able to do something. We therefore stop looking for solutions to accomplishing whatever we are considering and stay stuck where we are.

If you hear yourself say 'can't' or 'unable', repeat your sentence changing the words 'can't' or 'unable' to 'can'. If you don't believe that you 'can', ask, 'How can I...?' and brainstorm answers to this question, if they aren't immediately obvious. Appendix 3 gives guidance on how to perform effective brainstorming.

DON'T

The word 'don't' needs to be considered in two contexts:

1 **When we use the word 'don't' to mean we lack something that we want or need**, for example, 'I don't have enough time to write.' When used in this context, 'I don't' behaves in a similar way to when we say 'I can't' or 'I'm unable', by stopping us thinking that we might be able to have what we want. We therefore stop looking for solutions and stay stuck where we are.
   If you hear yourself say 'don't' in this context, repeat the sentence changing 'don't' to 'do' (or 'don't' to 'can', if this is more appropriate). If you don't believe this new positive sentence, ask, 'How can I...?' and brainstorm answers if they aren't immediately obvious. Appendix 3 gives guidance on how to perform effective brainstorming.
2 **When we use the word 'don't' in conjunction with something we want**, for example, if we break the habit of spending too much time checking emails, we might tell ourselves, 'I don't spend half the day checking emails any more.'
   Even though this is a positive action, we hear the 'don't' as a loss and it feels negative. In mentioning what we are not doing, we also remind ourselves of the habit we want to kick and tempt ourselves to return to it. A much better phrase to use would be one that tells you what you are doing instead of checking emails, such as writing.

WON'T/ONLY/LOSE

Just as when we use the word 'don't' in the second context earlier, 'won't', 'only' and 'lose' all give us a negative vibe even when we're using them to mean something positive. For example, 'I won't spend half of tomorrow tidying instead of writing.'

If you find yourself using these words when you are pleased about a situation, ask, 'What have I gained here?' and shift your focus to that instead.

FAIL

Thinking we failed is detrimental to both our motivation and our confidence. When you find yourself thinking or saying, 'I failed', remind yourself that we usually learn more from failure than success. Reflect on what you have learned from the experience and how you will use that learning to help you succeed in the future. Finally, focus your thoughts and energies on putting what you have learned into action.

PROBLEM

Identifying something as a 'problem' builds up the expectation that we have to deal with something negative and unpleasant that might get the better of us. Every time you hear yourself say 'problem', change it to the word 'challenge', which implies you are talking about something you can overcome and spurs you into questioning how you can beat it.

HARD/DIFFICULT

If we expect something to be hard, we are more likely to shrink back from doing it. Our attitude is also unlikely to be positive when we work on it. Again, the word 'challenge' is a good replacement. However, if you hear yourself thinking or saying something will be hard or difficult, also ask yourself, 'How could I make it easy?'

WISH

This is a great word if you see it as a positive, for example, when you make a wish or have a wish list. However if you hear yourself think or say, 'I wish…', check that you are not using wish in the context of something being out of your grasp, for example, 'I wish I had more time to write.' If you are, ask, 'How can I achieve or have this?'

IMPOSSIBLE

Thinking or saying something is impossible stops us seeing solutions. If you use this word, ask, 'Is it really impossible?' If it isn't impossible, then you need to identify what's making you think it is impossible and work on the challenge that reveals.

STUCK/BLOCKED/I HAVE WRITER'S BLOCK

As explained at the start of Chapter 7, your subconscious believes what you say and tries to help you act that way. If you say you're 'stuck', 'blocked', 'have writer's block' or any similar phrase, you will make it easier for yourself to remain that way. Chapter 12 discusses the idea of 'writer's block' and being 'blocked' more extensively.

NOT ENOUGH/RUNNING OUT/NONE

Every time you tell yourself you have none, not enough or you're running out of something, you tell yourself there's no point looking for more. Instead of using these words, tell yourself you can have or find more then go looking for it.

BUT

This identifies a reason, or several reasons, why you are not doing something.

When you hear yourself say 'but', ask, 'Is there any positive or insurmountable reason for not taking action to deal with this "but"?' Also ask, 'Am I happy to take responsibility for the possible consequences, if I do take action?'

If there isn't an insurmountable reason you cannot do something and you're happy to take responsibility for the possible consequences, you can address the 'but' and overcome it.

OUGHT, SHOULD, COULD, MUST OR HAVE TO

These words suggest you either know you need to do something, or you know someone else thinks you should do it, but you are holding back.

When you hear yourself say 'ought', 'should', 'could', 'must' or 'have to', ask, 'What are the reasons I ought/should/could/must/have to do this?'

- If there are good reasons to do it, place this activity on your own agenda as a 'need', 'want' or 'can do' and deal with whatever is causing resistance.
- If there are no good reasons, use the techniques discussed in Chapter 7 to remove the thought.

TRY, ATTEMPT OR HAVE A GO

When you say these words, you accept that you might fail a task before you have even started.

If you hear yourself say 'try', 'attempt' or 'have a go', counteract them by saying, 'I will do it', or 'I'm going to do it.'

- If this sits comfortably with you, work on changing your language to become positive.
- If your internal voice doubts your abilities, consider if it is telling you that you need to be better prepared or that the consequences of not succeeding are unacceptable to you. Take notice and take appropriate action.

Also remember that it's impossible to 'try' to do something. You either do it or you don't. If you remind yourself of this when you hear yourself say 'try', it can help encourage you to throw yourself fully into what you're doing or to step back and identify what further preparation you need to make.

AFRAID, FRIGHTENED, NERVOUS, SCARED OR ANY WORDS THAT DENOTE LACK OF CONFIDENCE

If you hear yourself saying, or thinking, anything that indicates fear or lack of confidence, these words are reminding you that you are stepping out of one of your comfort zones. Reflect on how you can reduce or remove your fear to make it easier to push the boundaries. However, remember the voice of fear is there to keep you safe. Always ensure you're happy to accept the consequences when you act against it.

Appendix 3

Effective brainstorming

1 Start by clearly identifying your challenge or the question you are seeking an answer to.
2 Relax – take yourself into the alpha brainwave state if possible. (See *Accessing the creative state* in Chapter 9 for further details on how to achieve this.)
3 Write down all and any answers you can think of to your challenge/question, applying the following rules:
   - Don't force out answers or think you have to come up with 'the right idea' straight away.
   - Quantity not quality is what you are aiming for – come up with as many answers as you can think of.
   - Do not judge any idea you come up with, just keep looking for more.
   - Aim to create as long a list as possible.
   - Aim to be creative in your solutions; ideas can be ridiculous, crazy or impossible – if you think of them just write them down.
   - One idea tends to trigger another, so if you think of a way of adding to, expanding or improving an idea, write it down.
   - Enjoy the process and have fun being creative.
4 Once you have created your list, reflect and consider if there are any ideas that you wish to use, or that you can modify to do something realistic, to overcome your challenge. Once more, work in a relaxed, creative mindset to help you find as many solutions as possible.
5 If your brainstorming session doesn't bring you any suitable solutions, treat it as the first step in a creative process of finding a solution. Do this by leaving the list for now, and coming back to consider it again later, or continuing to mull ideas over in your mind.
6 As you mull your thoughts over, or leave them for your subconscious to work on, remember that remaining detached

from finding a solution, and believing that you will find one, is the best way to increase your odds of finding a workable solution.

7 If you keep coming up with the same obstacle that prevents you from implementing the solutions you identify, brainstorm how you can remove that obstacle. Also consider if fear is holding you back and what you can do to address your concerns if it is.

Note

You might also find it helpful to ask a friend to help you identify solutions. However, if you share brainstorming it can actually reduce your chances of finding solutions, because you become more self-aware and may censor your suggestions, because of the presence of the other person.

Appendix 4

The Write Coach Survey

The survey referred to in Chapters 10, 12 and 14 was carried out between January 2 and January 17 2011. Of the 56 writers surveyed, 28 were unpublished, 26 were published and two were self-published.

Taking it further

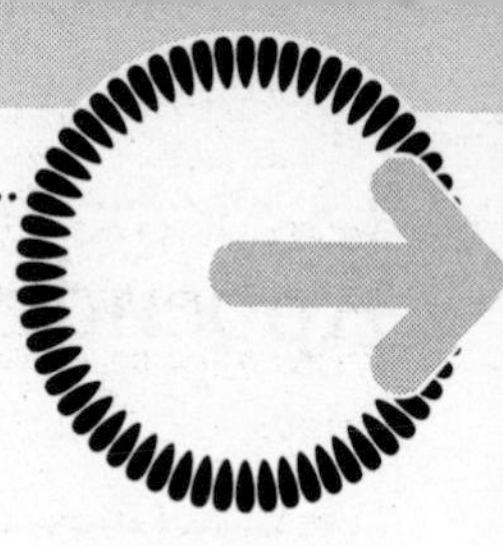

For further coaching tips, inspiration and news of my workshops visit my website www.thewritecoach.co.uk

Follow me on twitter @bekkiwritecoach

DEALING WITH LIMITING THINKING

Jeffers, S. (2011) *Feel the Fear and Do It Anyway*, Arrow
www.susanjeffers.com

CREATIVITY

Bell, J. and Magrs, P. (eds) (2001) *The Creative Writing Coursebook*, Macmillan
Writers tips, exercises and case studies used by MA students at UEA.

Cameron, J. (1997) *The Artists Way*, Pan Books
Spiritually based 12-week programme for enhancing creativity.

TIME

www.nanowrimo.com
Website for the annual (November) novel-writing project that brings together professional and amateur writers from all over the world.

www.picturebookmarathon.org
Website for the annual (February) picture book writing/illustrating project.

WRITING FICTION

Corner, H. and Weatherly, L. (2010) *How to Write a Blockbuster, Teach Yourself*, Hodder Education
A commercial approach to writing and submitting non-fiction.

Card, O. S. (1999) *Characters and Viewpoint*, Writer's Digest
Developing characters and viewpoints.

Field, S. (2005) *Screenplay: the foundations of screenwriting*, Bantam Dell
A commercial approach to writing screenplays.

Mckee, R. (1999) *Story*, Methuen
An in-depth look at the substance, style and structure of stories. Written for screenwriters, but an excellent book for all fiction writers.

Tobias, R. (2003) *20 Master Plots*, Walking Stick Press
Discusses story by considering 20 different plot structures.

Vogler, C. (2007) *The Writer's Journey*, Michael Wiese Production
Considers the relationship between mythology and storytelling in popular culture.

WRITING NON-FICTION

Larsen, M. (2004) *How to Write a Book Proposal*, Walking Stick Press

Stine, J. M. (1997) *Writing Successful Self-help and How-to Books*, John Wiley and Sons

GETTING PUBLISHED

Stock, R. (2005) *The Insider's Guide to Getting Published*, White Ladder Press

WRITER'S REFERENCE BOOKS

The Writers' and Artists' Yearbook, A&C Black
Children's Writers' and Artists' Yearbook, A&C Black
The Writer's Handbook, Macmillan
Reference books published annually containing advice, contacts, competitions, grants, courses and more.

WRITING MAGAZINES

The Bookseller
www.thebookseller.com
Leading trade magazine for the publishing world, published weekly.

Mslexia
www.mslexia.co.uk
High-quality fiction, interviews, contests, courses and writing information for women, published quarterly.

Writers' Forum
www.writers-forum.com
Monthly tips, information on contests, courses, etc.

Writers' News and *Writing Magazine*
www.writersnews.co.uk

Writers' News is subscription only, geared at prizes, competitions and writers' news.

Writing Magazine can be bought off the shelf. Offers monthly tips, interviews, information on competitions and courses.

WRITING GROUPS AND ASSOCIATIONS

The Crime Writers' Association
www.thecwa.co.uk
For published crime writers.

The Romantic Novelists' Association
www.rna-uk.org
For published and unpublished authors of romantic fiction.

The Society of Authors
www.societyofauthors.org
Support service for published writers and illustrators, but you can join once you have been offered a contract and the society will vet the contract free of charge.

The Society of Children's Book Writers and Illustrators (SCBWI)
www.scbwi.org

www.britishscbwi.jimdo.com
American-based organization for published and unpublished children's writers and illustrators. The British Isles region runs workshops, critique groups, has a quarterly newsletter and annual two-day conference.

National Association of Writers' Groups
www.nawg.co.uk
Find a writers' group in your area.

USEFUL WEBSITES/BLOGS

www.emmadarwin.typepad.com/about.html
Written by novelist, short story writer and tutor Emma Darwin.

www.helpineedapublisher.blogspot.com/
Written by the award-winning author of over 90 books, Nicola Morgan.

www.howpublishingreallyworks.com
A blog about the publishing industry.

www.notesfromtheslushpile.blogspot.com
A blog by various authors about writing for children, getting published and surviving the internet.

www.wordsunlimited.typepad.com
Writing prompts, book reviews and more from novelist, poet and writing tutor Pamela Johnson.

www.writers-circles.com
Directory of writers' circles, courses and websites.

www.writewords.org.uk
Online resource for writers.

Index